Technical Analysis
for
Financial Markets Traders

by
Jay and Julie Hawk

First edition.

Published by Jellyhawk Financial Press

Copyright © 2018 Jay and Julie Hawk

www.thefxperts.com

All rights reserved. This book or any portion thereof may not be reproduced or used in any manner whatsoever without the express written permission of the authors except for the use of brief quotations in a book review.

ISBN-13: 978-1984909343
ISBN-10: 1984909347

DEDICATION

This book is dedicated to our dear family who loved us, believed in us and encouraged us to excel in our chosen professions

JAY AND JULIE HAWK

TABLE OF CONTENTS

	Dedication	iii
	Table of Contents	v
	Acknowledgements	vii
	Foreword	ix
1	Introduction to Technical Analysis	Pg #1
2	Technical Analysis Techniques	Pg #7
3	Trading With Technical Analysis	Pg #31
4	Technical Analysis and Trading Software	Pg #43
5	Technical Indicators Explained	Pg #55
6	Recommended Further Reading	Pg #109
	About the Authors	Pg #113
	Glossary	Pg #117
	Index	Pg #125

JAY AND JULIE HAWK

ACKNOWLEDGMENTS

This book is the product of many years of personal experience and research obtained by working professionally in the financial markets, trading for our own accounts, and writing about trading as freelancers. We want to thank those who brought us up, those who taught us how to trade, and those who paid us to write for them.

JAY AND JULIE HAWK

FOREWORD

As long term professional experts and authors in the field of financial markets and derivatives trading, one of the most exciting things we have had the opportunity to witness personally in our careers was the electronification of the major financial markets and the advent of online forex, stock, commodity and CFD trading for retail speculators.

That important development meant a trader no longer had to be a high-net worth individual, producer, corporation or a market professional to buy and sell currency pairs, stocks or commodities, and they could far more efficiently trade such assets for profit from the convenience of their own homes and even from mobile devices.

Once that market evolution happened, almost anyone could then open up a margin trading account with an online Contract for Difference or CFD broker and trade CFDs speculatively on margin, even if they only had a small stake to put at risk. All they needed was a reasonably modern computer connected to the Internet that they could run an electronic trading platform on.

With relatively sophisticated trading and technical analysis software like MetaTrader available as a free download and a plethora of online brokers vying for retail business, this just made the financial markets even more accessible to virtually any person who wanted to get involved. This remarkable phenomenon notably changed the formerly structured and highly regulated world of financial markets trading dramatically. Now the general public wanted to try their hands at speculating on financial market movements too!

Over the years since that major market evolution occurred, we have been on the forefront of educating the increasingly savvy public about how to trade and analyze the various financial markets profitably. Even for many experienced traders, operating successfully in the financial markets can be a challenge due to the inherent volatility of market prices. Inexperienced traders were further hampered by their lack of knowledge about how to perform technical and fundamental analysis that they needed to understand in order to forecast future market prices with sufficient accuracy to be profitable when trading.

The harsh reality remains that without a solid foundation, most buildings do not last very long, and the same holds true for financial market traders. Without a solid educational foundation and a good working understanding of how the financial markets operate, how to analyze the markets, and how to make money consistently when trading, the margin accounts of most would-be traders are quickly depleted.

Knowing this all too well due to our professional trading backgrounds, we aimed to use our insider expertise to help such retail traders by writing widely on the subject for numerous Internet websites so that they could freely access this essential information. Working for over a decade as freelance writers, we have at this point contributed thousands of articles to this information pool, as well as online courses, e-books and reports. We even ghostwrote several published books on the subject of financial markets and derivatives that were attributed to other writers.

With this book on technical analysis, we offer the second in a two-part series of books on analyzing the financial markets aimed at traders. In it, we intend to share our knowledge and expertise in technical analysis — which is deeply relevant to operating successfully in each of the financial markets — with the public in a different format.

Our goal in publishing a book under our own names is to take a higher-profile role in educating prospective traders realistically about what is involved in analyzing financial markets in order to trade them profitably. We also aim to complement the background of more experienced traders with professional technical analysis methods and techniques that they may not yet be familiar with. Successful trading is not exactly easy, but it does not have to be overly difficult either, especially with access to the proper technical analysis tools and education.

This guide to technical analysis is designed to give traders and prospective traders a solid foundation to build upon as they operate in any of the financial markets. We intend to do this by sharing our insider knowledge about the different established technical analysis methods relevant for each of the financial markets that we are most intimately familiar with. We also provide a handy reference guide to understanding some of the more popular indicators used in technical analysis that traders who operate in virtually any market where prices are affected by supply and demand factors really need to know about.

The initial chapter of this book introduces the topic of technical analysis, discusses its basic premises, and compares it to the fundamental analysis methods that we cover in great detail in the first book in this two-part series. Subsequent chapters deal with how to perform technical analysis of the financial markets, which traders can typically use similar technical analysis methods to trade in each of them because their movements are based on human psychology.

The topic of automated trading is also brought up due to its growing significance in the modern era of trading robots and artificial intelligence, as well as the fact that almost all Expert Advisors decide when to trade based on technical analysis methods. That section is then then followed by a comprehensive reference guide covering each of the most popular technical indicators that technical analysts generally need to be familiar with. This section helps the reader understand, compute and use each technical indicator in practice to trade financial markets.

We then finish off the book by offering some helpful ideas for further reading that we found very valuable when we were starting our education on technical analysis and trading, as well as a bit of information about our professional backgrounds to establish our authority to educate on this subject and a glossary of commonly-used financial terms pertaining to technical analysis and the financial markets.

While the age-old trading goal of "buying low and selling high" continues to be the key when pursuing a profit in any financial market, having some decent insider knowledge under your belt about the principles of technical analysis and how to use them can really help you better discern what levels are high and what levels are low.

Nevertheless, while traders generally need to be aware of the technical analysis methods covered in this book, they do not need to overcomplicate their trading decisions by performing excessive amounts of technical analysis by hand, especially since many of the most successful trading plans and techniques can be quite simple and total automation is now an option for many technical traders. Unless you plan on using a trading robot, simple technical trading strategies are also often the most profitable since they are the easiest to apply quickly in a fast moving market, and traders using them can therefore capture more of the anticipated move.

Overall, we think this second book in our financial markets analysis series published by Jellyhawk Financial Press on technical analysis will make an excellent introduction and reference guide to what can appear to be a complicated subject. We do this by highlighting and explaining what traders really need to know about the rather broad topic of technical analysis, and we intended for this book to educate both novice and seasoned traders alike.

In concluding, we wish our readers great success in their financial trading careers and hope they enjoy them as much as we have ours.

Jay and Julie Hawk
www.thefxperts.com
Northern California, January, 2018

CHAPTER 1: INTRODUCTION TO TECNICAL ANALYSIS

Financial market analysis is generally performed to differentiate pure gambling or speculation from strategic trading. Performing this task allows a trader to determine a market's most likely future direction, whether higher, roughly the same, or lower.

This is done so that a trader can establish positions to profit from an accurate directional prediction, with long positions generally being established to profit from a market rise, while short positions would be taken to make money from a decline.

Technical indicators and charts showing price or exchange rate levels are some of the primary types of information reviewed by technical analysts. The analytical techniques in use remain fairly consistent between financial markets, and the most popular technical indicators are computed from market observables like price, volume and open interest for each asset.

While technical analysis cannot typically explain why a market moves, which generally lies in the domain of fundamental analysis that is covered in our first book in this financial markets analysis series, it can provide clear trade entry and exit signals that make its methods invaluable for a financial markets trader to time the execution of transactions.

Technical versus Fundamental Analysis

As you may already know, the two primary types of market analysis used by traders consist of fundamental and technical analysis. Fundamental analysis takes into account various material and immaterial factors that may affect an asset's market valuation and is generally most relevant to long term price movements.

In contrast, technical analysis focuses on variations and levels of market observables like price, volume and open interest. This form of analysis really helps traders time their market entry and exit points.

Since technical analysis focuses largely on an asset's price or exchange rate action and the behavior of other market observables like volume and open interest, as well as on indicators computed from them, using that analytical method can often be reduced to a set of rules that typically lends itself well to automation and inclusion into an objective trade plan.

In contrast, fundamental analysis usually requires a human to perform it due to its greater complexity and the need to make judgment calls about the relative importance of various factors and read news and other financial reports.

For these reasons, most traders use fundamental analysis to assess the reasons and causes for long term trends in practice, while also using technical analysis for timing market entry and exit points. This winning combination allows them to add an objective element to their trading plans when it comes to signaling the time to trade, while still grasping the big picture about why market movements are taking place.

Those traders interested in exploring fundamental analysis further are referred to the first volume of this market analysis series for traders written by the same authors and published by Jellyhawk Financial Press. That book, entitled "Fundamental Analysis for Financial Markets Traders", covers the various fundamental analysis methods and factors in great detail for the forex, stock and commodities markets, along with how to apply them properly in a trading environment.

Before this book covers the particulars of how to perform technical analysis for the various financial markets, it first makes sense to review some of the issues with relying solely on fundamental analysis as a financial markets trader and how technical analysis can help solve some of those problems.

How Technical Analysis Improves on Fundamental Analysis

In terms of the point of separation between the two disciplines of technical and fundamental analysis, it has already been noted that technicians rely primarily on price, volume and open interest data, as well as information derived from those market observables, as they evolve over time. Fundamental analysts, on the other hand, take into account just about everything else other than those factors.

Furthermore, when considering the relative merits of focusing on fundamental analysis versus the technical forms of market analysis, many seasoned traders note some serious issues both with the time and lack of objectively involved in performing fundamental analysis and also with its effectiveness as a technique for forecasting near term price moves.

The rest of this section contains a discussion of some of their more common issues seen with applying fundamental analysis to trading the financial markets and how technical analysis can help resolve some of these problems.

Fundamentals Take Time

When it comes to performing an analysis to obtain a currency forecast, a fundamental analyst usually has to review a far greater set of information than the technical analyst. Since time is money in the financial markets, and trading opportunities can easily be missed if prompt action is not taken, any delay in pulling the trigger on a trade can have a significant adverse impact on your trading business.

For example, a forex fundamental analyst might have to look over a slew of economic data for the country of each currency in a currency pair, plus take into account interest rate, inflation, purchasing power parity, and growth differentials, as well as supply and demand effects, political influences, geopolitical events and relevant commodity prices. Stock and commodity market analysis can get even more involved, since additional things like balance sheets or even weather forecasts will often be reviewed when performing fundamental analysis.

Basically, the task of performing a comprehensive fundamental analysis for a financial market asset can get quite daunting, especially for those without strong analytical training and an economic background. As a result, fundamentals-based traders can easily get left behind and stuck deep in analysis paralysis, while the market technician may have already performed their analysis and moved appropriately into the market in a more timely fashion, and they may even have automated their trading plan entirely.

Lack of Specific Trade Recommendations

Most technical analysts have developed and follow in a disciplined way one or more clearly-defined trade plans. These sets of trading guidelines tell them valuable and objective information about what to look for, when to enter the market, and at what levels positions should be liquidated at a profit or loss. Technical trade plans also usually incorporate money management principles that tell the trader how to size their trades, generally depending on their risk tolerance and portfolio size.

Unfortunately, fundamental analysts usually do not enjoy the advantage of having such clear trade plans. It can be difficult to incorporate all of the information they need to review into a specific trade recommendation with pre-defined entry and exit points. The resulting lack of objectivity can often make the difference between a financial markets trader being successful or not.

All News is Old News

The idea behind this issue with fundamental analysis is that any news released to the public has pretty much already been noted, analyzed and fully discounted into the exchange rate by professional market-makers. Such people specialize in quoting prices in a particular asset and change their prices as soon as news is released to reflect updated valuation information.

Basically, their intense job requires them to keep their fingers right on the pulse of the market using rapid market data services, news wires and the market's own well-developed rumor-mill. Large traders might even establish directional positions ahead of the fact to profit from expected movements based on rumors, large anticipated transactions or their own in-house valuation analysis.

As a result, traders looking to take positions based on fundamentals will often be sorely frustrated to see the market react to news in a thoroughly counter-intuitive way as the market pros "buy the rumor and sell the fact."

Why Technical Analysis Works

Those new to trading may wonder why technical analysis works so well to predict future levels of asset prices or exchange rates. They might question why just looking at the basic price data, chart patterns or trading volume levels over time can have any predictive value whatsoever.

They might also not understand how to use the various technical indicators that involve quantitatively assessing some aspect of how prices change, or why such indicators can yield useful trading signals.

This healthy sort of skepticism makes perfect sense to novice traders first exposed to the more advanced topic of technical analysis. Nevertheless, many more experienced traders swear by the effectiveness and efficiency of using technical analysis in predicting future directional movements in prices and forex rates.

As a result, technical analysis and its plethora of technical indicators have taken a permanent place aside fundamental economic analysis and economic indicators as an established way of looking at and forecasting future market movements.

The rest of this section discusses the theoretical basis for using technical analysis to trade financial markets.

An Explanation

Although many people have attempted to explain why technical analysis works, often in quite different ways, perhaps the best explanation arises from the idea that prices in asset markets and the exchange rates seen in the forex market represent the equilibrium point at which buying pressure equals selling pressure for the market involved. If either buyers or sellers start to predominate, the market will move appropriately.

Furthermore, the flow of information into the consciousness of the market's many participants tends to occur efficiently as a result of news services and real-time pricing. As a result, the forex rates seen in the currency market, for example, generally respond rapidly to new economic and political events as they occur, and they even take into account or "discount" events that are rumored to be about to occur.

In practice, this means that financial markets soon discount all of the available information pertaining to each asset traded in them, and they do this efficiently and on a continuous basis. This general concept underlies what a technical analyst intends to communicate when they say: "Price discounts all."

Why Read the News?

Most personal traders do not have the time, information systems, background or inclination to be reading detailed economic reports, scanning news wires for the latest news flashes or constantly having their finger on the pulse of the market like a professional market-maker might need to in order to keep their jobs. They generally want to have a life instead.

Using technical analysis can provide a workable solution for such armchair traders. All they have to do is make the reasonable assumption that all such available information gets quickly priced into the market by the trading pros whose job it is to do so. After all, why second guess the experts?

This really takes the pressure off when it comes to watching the news. Basically, observed market levels will most likely not change as an inexperienced trader might expect based on the old news they have access to because the information has probably already been discounted by the professional market makers. As the old saying goes, the pros generally "Buy the rumor, and sell the fact."

Human Behavior Repeats Itself

Besides the assumption that the prevailing market levels take into account all available relevant information, the other fundamental reason why technical analysis works has to do with the repeatability, and hence the predictability, of human behavior when people act as a group.

The crowd mentality seen operating in virtually any financial marketplace tends to demonstrate certain patterns of behavior, which in turn show up visually in exchange rate or price movements as they are plotted over time.

Since these observable patterns tend to repeat themselves time and time again, the results can help forecast the future behavior of a market. While that may indeed be true, the trick to this form of technical analysis lies in correctly identifying which pattern the market is trading in.

CHAPTER 2: TECHNICAL ANALYSIS TECHNIQUES

In any introduction to the techniques and methods used in technical analysis, perhaps the first thing a trader needs to understand is that fundamental information like economic data and interest rate differentials become rapidly priced or "discounted" into a market once they are commonly available to market-makers. The saying that technical traders often use to encapsulate this key concept is: "Price discounts all."

As discussed in the previous chapter, the art and science of technical analysis assumes the truth of this idea, in addition to making the observation that human behavior in crowds tends to repeat itself. Such behavior shows up visually in the price action observed over time as market psychology fluctuates between periods of optimism or bullishness and pessimism or bearishness.

As a result of the foregoing assumptions, a trader basing their decisions on technical analysis can ignore all of the otherwise distracting market information. Instead, they can focus their attention on using the exchange rate or price and its past behavior to forecast its future direction, often with impressively accurate results.

The rest of this section outlines why and how technical analysis helps financial market traders, including an introductory discussion of chart patterns, trends, price levels and indicators that are among the more popular technical analysis techniques used by financial markets traders.

Chart Patterns

Another advantage of technical analysis arises from the fact that many so-called chart patterns provide specific "measuring objectives" in terms of price and even sometimes with respect to time when a particular trigger level is broken. As a result, once they identify a reliable chart pattern, the technical trader can operate in the markets with a considerably greater degree of objectivity.

In general, chart patterns tend to fall into the basic categories of continuation, reversal or consolidation patterns, depending on how the subsequent price action usually proceeds once the pattern completes itself.

Trends and Channels

Trends form an especially important class of continuation chart pattern. Technical analysts generally identify an uptrend by a series of higher highs and higher lows, and a down trend by a set of lower lows and highs. Furthermore, sets of parallel lines can sometimes be drawn through the identifying high and low reversal points to form a channel.

Once the price or exchange rate breaks an established channel in a direction contrary to the initial trend, that event signals the end of the trend. It also sets up a rate objective equal to the width of the channel projected from the point of penetration.

Support and Resistance

By looking at a chart of exchange rate or price movements over time, a technical analyst can identify places where buying interest overcame selling interest to prompt a bullish reversal in rate action, or where selling interest surpassed buying interest to prompt a bearish reversal.

These levels would be known as support and resistance levels respectively, because buying interest supports the market, while selling interest generally provides resistance to a move higher.

Technical Indicators

Another major area of technical analysis involves using one or more of the wide variety of technical indicators available to analyze exchange rate, price or volume data with numerically. Such indicators usually provide clear trading signals that traders often incorporate into their trader plans.

An example of one of the more popular indicators is the Relative

Strength Index. The RSI gives insight into whether the market is oversold or overbought and hence due for a consolidation or reversal. While infrequently used on its own, it can be used to confirm other technical signals by giving an indication of market momentum.

Useful Chart Patterns

As mentioned briefly in the previous section, useful chart patterns tend to fall into the basic categories of continuation, consolidation and reversal patterns. The classification of a chart pattern into these categories depends on how the subsequent market movement usually proceeds once the pattern completes itself.

Triangles present something of an exception because they can break out in either direction, and so can be either continuation or reversal patterns. These categories and some of the useful chart patterns within them that can help traders profit from their forecasts are described further below:

Continuation and Consolidation Patterns

As the name implies, a continuation pattern is one that signals that the market will continue again in the same direction once the pattern has completed. These patterns could also be called consolidation patterns since they tend to represent a pause in the general direction of the market as it consolidates after its recent move. Volume tends to decrease as the market takes a temporary breather, and it then rises again upon a breakout. Examples of common continuation patterns include:

- **Triangles** – These patterns come in symmetrical, ascending and descending types. The market typically trades in a gradually narrower range as it consolidates between converging trend lines before breaking out on increased volume and continuing in that direction.

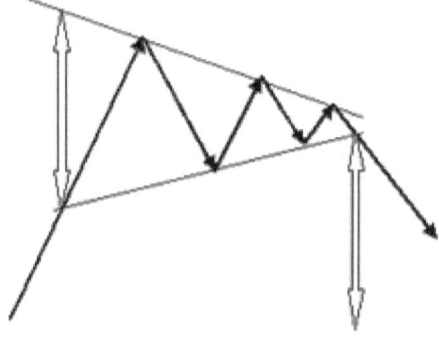

Although certainly a consolidation pattern, as noted earlier, a triangle can be either a continuation or a reversal pattern, depending on which side its breakout occurs on.

Triangles also generally consist of five increasingly smaller internal movements, and they must break out before reaching their apex. A breakout sets up measuring objective equal to the width between the converging trend lines that define the pattern at the initial high or low.

- **Flags** - Preceded by a sharp move, often called the "flag-pole", the market consolidates between parallel trend lines that often slant counter-trend, before resuming sharply in its original direction, and to a similar extent to the original move.

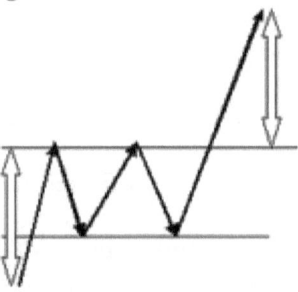

- **Pennants** – Also preceded by a sharp "flag-pole" move, the market consolidates between converging trend lines, usually resembling a small symmetrical triangle, before resuming sharply in its original direction and to a similar extent to the original move.

- **Wedges** – Consists of two converging trend lines. A falling wedge interrupts an uptrend, and its breakout is bullish, while a rising wedge interrupts a down trend and its breakout is bearish.

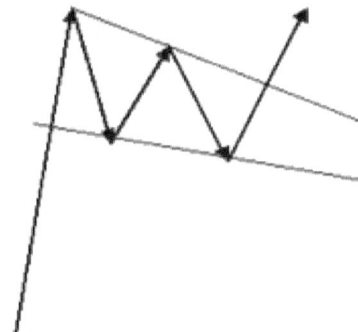

- **Rectangles** – A trading range bordered by roughly horizontal lines drawn among the major highs on the top and among the major lows on the bottom. A breakout in either direction sets up a measured move equal to the width of the rectangle.

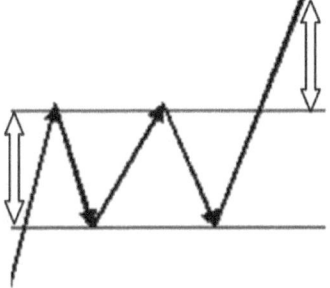

Reversal Patterns

Signs of a reversal pattern forming provide a good clue that the market may be about to turn and move in the opposite direction. Examples of common reversal patterns include:

- **Head and Shoulders Top or Bottom** – One shoulder forms, then a head forms a major top or bottom, then another shoulder appears at a similar level to the first. The dips or rallies between the head and the shoulders define a neckline. When the neckline breaks, look for a move equal to the distance between the neckline and the head.

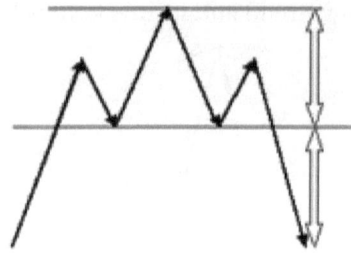

- **Double Top or Bottom** – Forms when two tests of a roughly similar level occur, with an intervening dip or rally. The dip/rally defines the neckline and a break of that level sets up a measured move equal to the distance between the neckline and the double peak/trough.

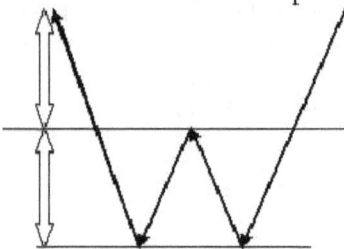

- **Triple Top or Bottom** – This pattern is like the double top or bottom, but with three peaks or troughs instead of two.

- **Triangles** – See the previous entry under continuation patterns for triangles which become reversal patterns when their breakout comes in the opposite direction to the preceding trend.

Trends, Trend Lines and Channels

By correctly identifying trends as they occur on charts, an experienced technical analyst can often use that information to assist them in forecasting the future market direction for that particular asset.

Not only can trends give technical analysts a valuable glimpse into the future, but such helpful chart patterns can also provide objective trading opportunities when they set up so-called "measuring objectives."

The rest of this section discusses the process of identifying trends, how to draw trend lines, and how traders use them to profit from directional movements in the financial markets.

Advantages of Trading Trends

One of the primary advantages of looking for trends on price or exchange rate charts arises from their tendency to point to the future direction of the market. Naturally, this provides a very useful piece of information from which traders can readily profit.

As the old market saying goes, "The trend is your friend," and many traders take this advice to heart by looking to position themselves to benefit from a continuation in the trend. If the trend heads higher, trend-following traders look to buy on dips, if the trend declines, they look to sell rallies.

Drawing Trend Lines

Drawing trend lines requires a technical analyst to first visually identify that a trend or directional movement exists or is in the process of forming. They do this by first making graphs that plot the price or exchange rate as it progresses over time for a certain asset. They then look for the market to make a series of higher highs and lows, when engaged in an upwards trend, or a series of lower lows and highs, when proceeding in a downwards trend.

In general, correctly drawing trend lines usually means connecting two or more of the major highs seen on a price graph with an upper line in the case of a downtrend, and two or more of the major lows with a lower line in the case of an upwards trend.

Market trends can be readily identified using this technique and then watched as the market progresses by drawing trend lines on real time charts and then saving them for later retrieval.

Channels

Furthermore, sometimes both upper and lower trend lines can be drawn around price action in the same direction that appear to parallel each other approximately. In this case, they together form an important chart pattern called a channel that tends to contain the price or exchange rate movements while the market remains within that trend.

This chart pattern provides a trading opportunity where traders will often look to buy when the market approaches the lower line of the channel, with their stops just below that line. Similarly, they will also look to sell when the market trades toward the upper channel line, and they will usually set their stops just above that line.

The End of the Trend

Furthermore, once the market price or exchange rate breaks either a well-established single trend line or a channel of parallel trend lines in a direction contrary to the initial trend, that event signals the end of the trend. It therefore pays to keep track of the levels of the major trend lines that fall near the current market levels as time progresses in order to know whether that particular trend has finished or remains in play.

In addition, when the market moves outside a well-established trend channel in a direction contrary to that trend, it generates a channel break signal. Such a signal sets up a "measuring objective," or an expected market move, that equals the width of the channel projected from the point at which the channel was convincingly broken.

Support and Resistance Levels

A chart that graphs price or exchange rate movements for a particular asset as a function of time can be a trader's best friend when it comes to identifying optimum places to buy and sell. Experienced technical analysts will scour such charts looking for significant points on the chart where the rate paused before continuing, reversed its direction entirely or where some other reason indicates the level may be difficult to break.

If a significant chart point appears below the market, it would be considered a support point since buyers often select such points to purchase and this activity tends to support the market. On the other hand, if such a point appears above the prevailing market, it would be termed a resistance point since sellers aggregating around that exchange rate level will tend to provide resistance to a move higher.

Traders, especially those employing range-trading strategies, often seek to identify such points so that they can buy ahead of support, with stops placed just below, and sell ahead of resistance, with stops placed just above.

The rest of this section discusses how professional traders go about determining support and resistance points on price or exchange rate charts.

Types of Support and Resistance

The price or exchange rate chart for a particular asset commonly displays several different types of levels that can help a trader in determining support and resistance to market movements. These might include:

- **Reversals** – the level at which the market stops moving in whatever direction it was going in and turns back. Look for major tops and bottoms on the chart, as well as shorter-term reversals within an overall recent trend.

- **Congestion** – typically consists of areas where the market pauses before continuing to move further in the direction it was originally heading. Sometimes, congestion might also arise from a number of reversals all occurring in the same general region on a chart.

- **Psychological Levels** – these are round numbers, in terms of the market quotation, that tend to provide psychological targets that longer-term players might use to move into or out of the market at. For example, psychological levels often have importance in currencies in which the USD is not the base currency. Such levels might include 1.5000 in GBP/USD and 1.2000 in EUR/USD, 100.00 in USD/JPY, and 1.0000 in AUD/USD.

- **Support Turned Resistance and Resistance Turned Support** – On occasion, the market will gather enough steam to push through a major support or resistance level. In this case, a broken support point will tend to become resistance as traders who bought ahead of it might look to close out for flat, while a bested resistance point will tend to become support.

- **Significant Trend Lines** - When a trend line can be clearly drawn through a set of higher lows in the case of an uptrend or a series of lower lows, in the case of a down trend, that trend line tends to provide support for the market at the point where the line crosses the current time. Similarly, when a trend line can be drawn through a series of lower highs, or higher highs, it creates resistance.

- **Fibonacci Retracement Levels** – When a major move has an important Fibonacci retracement level or Fibonacci projection point at a certain price or exchange rate, that level can tend to impede market movement, often forming support if below the current market or resistance if above. A more in-depth discussion of these important levels will follow in a later section.

Reading Candlestick Charts

As one of the most widely-used charting systems when it comes to analyzing the market, reading candlestick charts has become a daily pastime for many forex traders.

This important innovation was initially developed by Homma Munehisa in the 18th century. A legendary rice trader from Japan who traded Ojima rice in Sakata, Munehisa is considered one of the most successful traders in history. He generated the current dollar equivalent of over $100 billion in trading profits in his trading career, sometimes making $10 billion in a single year.

Around the year 1900, Charles Dow, an American technical analyst and the trader that put the "Dow" in Dow-Jones, adopted Munehisa's charting technique, and it has been used extensively ever since. The following sections contain a brief introduction to candlestick charts and an explanation on how to read them.

Candlestick Charts and How they Work

A normal bar chart gives the open, high, low and close of the market for each time period charted. In addition to that information, a candlestick chart also visually indicates whether the financial instrument or commodity closed up or down by using different color bars drawn between the high and low. Often these bars are colored red and green or sometimes black and white, as shown in the chart below.

The candlestick figure provides a useful snapshot picture of the trading activity that occurred over a set period of time. It consists of a white or filled-in box denoting if the price was up or down for the period. The candlestick figure includes:

- **An upper shadow or line** – this vertical line ends at the market's high which is at the top of the upper range for the period in question.

- **A body** – consists of a box which has the opening price at the bottom of the box and the closing price at the top of the box. If the box is not filled in, this indicates an up period. If the box is filled in, the box indicates a down period. The opening price sits at the top of the box and the bottom of the box is the closing price level.

- **A lower shadow** – this vertical line denotes the low for the period that was the maximum downward extent of the currency's range.

Candlestick Types

Candlesticks vary considerable in shape depending on the action in the market. For example, a long white candle with small upper and lower shadows indicates strong buying pressure in the market. While a black candle with the same attributes means the opposite, strong selling pressure.

Certain candlesticks have special names such as the:

- **Doji** – a formation that indicates a market reversal. It shows the same opening and closing price and appears like a cross, with the upper and lower shadows showing the range.

  Doji formations can be "long legged" meaning the trading range was large, or "Dragonfly", meaning the open and close were the same but the currency traded substantially lower.

  Also the "Tombstone" Doji occurs when the market went substantially higher but closed where it opened on the low of the period.

- **Marubozu** – a formation without upper or lower shadows with either a white or black body showing great buying or selling pressure.

- **Spinning Tops** – a candlestick with a long upper and lower shadow and a short body, which indicates indecision in the market.

Numerous other named candlesticks formations exist, and when particular combinations occur, technical analysts commonly interpret them to have certain implications for the market's future. Nevertheless, going into further depth on the subject lies beyond the scope of this book, so the reader is referred to an outside reference on candlestick charting and interpretation for more details on additional patterns.

Fortunately, many resources on reading candlestick charts can be found online, and a number of excellent books have been written on the subject to help further your research into this very interesting and useful chart pattern interpretation method.

Point and Figure Charts

Although not as commonly used among today's personal forex traders, the point and figure chart has been a technical analysis staple among professional traders for many years.

Among spot forex traders, this chart would be painstakingly constructed throughout the trading day as such traders listened intently to spot prices trading as they were announced through their forex brokers' voice boxes and then quickly noted down reversal points as they occurred.

These point and figure charts would usually be made by hand on pieces of graph paper that eventually got taped together and folded to form a detailed map of the market's many reversal points.

Times and methods may have changed since the advent of electronic trading and real-time price charts, but it would truly be a shame to let this especially useful charting technique go the way of the dinosaur.

Point and Figure Chart Benefits

A unique characteristic of a point and figure chart involves the lack of any time frame occurring in the chart since both axes of the chart depend on price alone. Furthermore, some of the advantages of point and figure charts include:

- Simplicity of construction.
- Only price matters since time does not get charted.

- Only price reversals of a chose size matter, which smoothes the chart.
- Common patterns generate clear buy and sell signals.
- Trends become easy to identify.
- Price objectives can be easily computed.

Useful Point and Figure Chart Patterns

By looking for common patterns that show up on point and figure charts, a trader experienced in reading them can readily generate buy and sell signals for an asset that allow them to trade with greater objectivity. Furthermore, traders can easily calculate price objectives by using either a vertical or horizontal box counting technique.

The names of some of the more useful point and figure chart patterns and their resulting trade signals follow:

- **Buy Signals:** Generally a higher bottom, then a higher top.
    - Double Top
    - Triple Top
    - Spread Triple Top
    - Bullish Triangle
    - Bullish Catapult
    - Long Tail Down
    - Low Pole

- **Sell Signals:** Generally a lower top, then a lower bottom.
    - Double Bottom
    - Triple Bottom
    - Spread Triple Bottom
    - Bearish Triangle
    - Bearish Catapult
    - High Pole

Constructing a Point and Figure Chart

Making a point and figure chart by hand will require a piece of graph paper, something to write with and access to traded exchange rates or prices. Once you have those elements, the rest of the steps become relatively easy and go roughly as follows:

1. Step 1: Select a "point" or unit of price to be represented by a single box on the graph paper.

2. Step 2: Place an "X" in a box to indicate upward movement or an "O" to indicate downward movement.

3. Step 3: Start a new column when a price reversal of three points or more occurs.

These days, traders will typically use charting software programmed to create point and figure charts. Although the popular MetaTrader trading platform does not include point and figure charts among its chart types, you can program an add-on to construct them using its price feed.

The image below is an example of how such an add-on displays a point and figure chart in MetaTrader with green boxes (show in lighter grey) representing rises and red boxes (shown in darker grey) declines.

Trading With the Trend

Even though a buy or sell signal might be generated, a trader observing it might still choose to refrain from following any signal that did not agree with the direction of the underlying trend. After all, "the trend is your friend", as the popular market saying goes.

Traders can readily use a point and figure chart to assess this trend factor for a bullish or rising market by drawing a 45-degree line upwards from the point of the previous major low. Any sell signals seen above this line would then be ignored, while buy signals would be taken.

For a bearish or falling market, a similarly-slanted line would be drawn downwards from the preceding major high. Any buy signals occurring above this line would be overlooked, but sell signals would be traded on.

Pivot Points

Although traditionally especially popular with floor traders due to their computational simplicity, pivot points also provide a useful trading signal methodology for desk traders. One of the main advantages of using pivot point analysis comes from the fact that it often has some useful predictive value, while most other technical indicators tend to lag behind the market.

The pivot point itself is determined by computing the simple average of the previous day's high, low and closing rates. Three sets of theoretical support and resistance levels can then readily be derived from that information.

The rest of this section discusses how to perform the pivot point calculations, as well as how traders use them to trade the financial markets effectively and even generate trading signals.

Calculating Pivot Points

Calculating each of the pivot point levels just requires the High, Low and Close prices for the previous period. The equation looks like this:

Central Pivot Point (Pivot) = (High + Low + Close) / 3

You then calculate theoretical support and resistance levels around this pivot point with the following formulas:

First Levels:

First Resistance (R1) = 2*Pivot - Low

First Support (S1) = 2*Pivot - High

Second Levels:

Second Resistance (R2) = Pivot + (R1-S1)

Second Support (S2) = Pivot - (R1- S1)

Third Levels:

Third Resistance (R3) = High + 2*(Pivot-Low)

Third Support (S3) = Low - 2*(High - Pivot)

Then you would plot horizontal lines at each of these seven levels on a chart of the price or exchange rate as it evolves over time.

Trading Pivot Points

The most important pivot point levels used when trading are the R1 and S1 levels, in addition to the key central pivot point. The other support and resistance points generally seem best used for profit-taking.

When using pivot points in practice, traders would first observe the level of the market at the open. If the market opens above the central pivot, then the sentiment is bullish and long trades will be preferred.

Conversely, an open below the pivot point indicates a bearish outlook, with a resulting preference for establishing short positions.

Pivot Point Trading Signals

Traders will generally watch for a break of the R1 or S1 levels to signal the direction in which to take a position. They might also confirm such a break using another indicator like a set of moving averages.

In terms of the actual trade signals used when trading pivot points, if R1 breaks then a pivot point trader would tend to go long, but if S1 breaks they would instead prefer to short the market. Sell stops on longs would usually be placed under R1, while buy stops on shorts would be entered above S1.

When the market eventually goes up to R2 or R3 or down to S2 or S3, it will already tend to be overbought or oversold respectively. As a result, the R2, R3, S2, S3 levels are usually used as exit points for profit taking, instead of as additional entry points.

Elliott Wave Theory

Some of the most interesting techniques that fall under the umbrella of technical analysis are those that form the application of Elliott Wave Theory that was developed by R.N. Elliott.

Using technical analysis techniques based on Elliott Wave Theory can be a valuable way to analyze virtually any financial market since it allows a trader to understand the bigger picture of how a market is evolving over time. Not only can such traders gain market insights that no other analytic technique can offer, but the fractal nature of the Theory means they can even make market forecasts for a variety of different time frames.

In practice, a trader skilled in applying Elliott Wave Theory can obtain directional guidance, reasonable price objectives and clear stop-loss levels from a detailed analysis using its techniques. Furthermore, many traders do not realize they already use a technique based on Elliott Wave Theory when they compute Fibonacci retracement and projection objectives that will be covered in greater detail in the subsequent section.

The rest of this section contains an introduction to Elliott Wave Theory and several tips and techniques for applying it to profitably trade the financial markets.

The Basics of Elliot Wave Theory

In expounding his traditional Wave Theory, R.N. Elliott proposed that a series of five waves were typically observed in market trends. He numbered these waves one through five, where the odd-numbered waves that furthered the trend were called impulses, while the even-numbered waves that moved against the trend were called corrections.

After that initial five-wave sequence, the trend itself corrects in the opposite direction to the trend. Corrections usually unfold in a series of three or five waves that Elliott used letters to denote. Such corrections could be:

- **Zig-Zags** - sharp three-wave corrections with a 5-3-5 wave internal structure.

- **Flats** – more consolidative three-wave corrections with a 3-3-5 structure.

- **Triangles** – consolidative five-wave corrections with a 3-3-3-3-3 structure.

Overall, this results in a classic eight-wave sequence of trend and correction that Elliott postulated played itself out over and over again on a cyclical basis for both long and short time frames as the market progressed over time.

Furthermore, since Elliott and those using his Theory generally first look at market activity and then "count" waves to see where the market is unfolding in this sequence, analysts commonly refer to this as a "wave count."

Fibonacci Retracements and Projections

Elliott later enhanced his Wave Theory in the 1940's by using ratios based on the famous Fibonacci sequence to calculate likely correction targets for market retracements and to project probable objectives for impulses. Collectively, traders now refer to these as Fibonacci retracement and projection levels.

For determining likely retracement targets, analysts now commonly use ratios of 1:0.236, 1:0.382, 1:0.500, 1:0.618 and 1:1.764. The 1 represents the initial move now subject to correction.

For computing projection targets, analysts often use ratios of 1:1, 1:1.236, 1:1.382, 1:1.618, 1.764, 1:2, and so on. The 1 refers to the length of the initial move to be followed by another move with a length related to the first by a Fibonacci ratio.

Putting Elliott's Wave Theory into Practice

When applying Elliott Wave Theory, technicians tend to go through the following four basic steps:

(1) First review exchange rate movements seen in the target currency pair over the time frame they have an interest in analyzing watching for completed three- or five-wave sequences that can yield a starting point.

(2) Compile a series of possible alternative wave counts that take into account the observed exchange rate activity.

(3) Look for any incomplete structures, and compute target Fibonacci retracement objectives and projections as appropriate.

(4) Wait until one wave count emerges as a high-probability scenario from which to project future market action and then use this count to influence their trading.

Overall, applying Elliott Wave Theory when trading forex means carefully reviewing the forex charts of the currency pairs you want to trade, and waiting patiently for a clear wave count picture to arise. Only then will using this advanced technical analysis technique give you the ability to foresee the market's future that so many traders seek.

Fibonacci Retracements

As touched upon in the previous section, the use of characteristics of the mathematical Fibonacci sequence to calculate market price retracement objectives was pioneered by R.N. Elliott when he enhanced his Wave Theory with this concept in the early 1940's.

In doing so, Elliott tied in his observation that mass human psychology was reflected in a classic eight-wave sequence commonly seen in market price action with the natural evolutionary sequence Fibonacci invented in relation to the reproduction of rabbits.

His basic conclusion was that market corrections tended to retrace their preceding trend according to set percentages of the length of that trend, and that those percentages in turn consist of ratios of successive numbers in the Fibonacci sequence.

Although many traders now use Fibonacci retracement levels regularly when looking to trade market corrections, not all of them know that they are applying an aspect of Elliott Wave Theory in doing so.

The Fibonacci Sequence and Ratios

The now-famous Fibonacci sequence was originally published in the early 13th century and involved a mathematical solution to a question posed about the reproduction of rabbits. A short-cut to calculating the series starts with 1 and 1 and then progresses by adding together the preceding two numbers to get the next number, and so on.

This process produces the infinite Fibonacci sequence as follows:

1, 1, 2, 3, 5, 8, 13, 21, 34, 55, 89, 144…

Mathematicians have observed several interesting things about ratios of numbers in this sequence that Elliott later proposed could be used to trade corrections. These include:

(1) The ratio of one number in the sequence, when divided by the next, approaches the so-called Golden Mean of 0.618.
(2) The ratio of one number in the sequence to the number two places further up approaches 0.382.
(3) The ratio of one number to the number three places down the sequence approaches 0.236.

Fibonacci Retracement Levels

Those observations, when expressed as percentages, result in the classic Fibonacci Retracement levels of 23.6%, 38.2% and 61.8%. Many Elliott Wave Theorists complete this retracement series by adding the 50%, the 100%-23.6% = 76.4%, and the 100% retracement levels, to obtain a retracement series based on the Fibonacci sequence as follows:

23.6%, 38.2%, 50%, 61.8%, 76.4% and 100%.

When an initial market trend occurs and the market then shows signs of beginning a correction or retracement in the opposite direction, an Elliot Wave Theorist will compute these percentages of the length of the initial impulse to yield a succession of retracement targets for the correction.

Trading Fibonacci Retracement Levels

In general, once one Fibonacci retracement level has been broken, that sets up the next Fibonacci retracement level as the subsequent target. Also, when the key 61.8% retracement level is broken, the correction will often return to the beginning of the preceding trend.

A Fibonacci Retracement level example calculation could involve a scenario where the AUD/USD rate has trended from 0.8000 to 0.9000. Once this initial move corrects over 23.6% of its length or:

$$0.9000 - 0.8000 = 0.1000 * 23.6\% = 0.0236,$$

then that would imply AUD/USD has pulled back from its high to a rate of:

0.9000 - 0.0236 = 0.8764.

A forex trader using Fibonacci retracements levels might then reasonably expect that the market will continue to correct lower provided that the market remains below this 23.6% level at 0.8764. If they were then to establish a short position in AUD/USD to take advantage of this correction, they would tend to place their buy stops above this level.

This procedure would generally be followed through successive Fibonacci retracement percentages as the exchange rate corrected lower until the market eventually reversed the correction as it began to move higher again and resume its upward trend. This would be signaled by a breach of the 23.6% retracement level at 0.8764. Profits would usually be taken on shorts ahead of each Fibonacci level in the correction sequence.

Popular Technical Indicators

One of the most popular methods of signaling trade entries and exits that falls within the realm of technical analysis involves the computation of indicators from market observables like price, volume and open interest. Due to the objectivity provided to traders by the use of technical indicators, most will incorporate signals based on one or more of the more popular indicators mentioned in this section in their trade plans.

Technical trading generally involves developing an objective trade plan that lays out in detail how trades will be entered and exited based on technical factors, like indicator readings for example. Traders will then typically use or develop signal criteria based on such indicators and then monitor the various markets being traded for signals to enter or exit trades.

While many standardized technical indicators exist, and some sophisticate traders even develop their own indicators, this section will focus on describing some of the most helpful and commonly-used technical indicators and how they can be used to generate trading signals.

Although each of these indicators will be covered in much greater detail in Chapter 5 of this book, along with quite a few others, the rest of this section will briefly introduce the more popular technical indicators and how to use them to trade financial markets.

Relative Strength Index or RSI

The RSI tells a technician whether a market is trading in oversold or overbought territory, and hence might be due for a period of correction or consolidation.

An RSI reading of 70 or greater indicates the market is overbought, while a level of 30 or less gives an oversold signal.

Moving Averages

Calculating moving averages of exchange rates smoothes and slows the action so that short-term fluctuations disappear and the longer-term trend becomes clearer. Technical analysts often compare the current exchange rate to its 200-day Moving Average to ascertain whether the long-term trend is up or down.

Also, trading signals can be generated by observing crossovers among moving averages of short and longer time periods. When the short term moving average crosses from below to above the long term, a buy signal is generated, and vice versa for a sell signal.

MACD (Moving Average Convergence/ Divergence)

This indicator shows the difference between short and longer term moving averages, with a crossover in the central (zero) region generating a trading signal.

If the MACD crosses from negative to positive, then that would generate a buy signal, and if the MACD went from positive to negative, then that would indicate a sell.

Historical Volatility

Volatility measures market risk due to past exchange rate swings, and historical volatility is calculated as the annualized standard deviation of observed price changes over some given time period, often 20 or 30 days.

The higher this indicator, the more risky the market has been to trade over the time period included in its calculation.

Bollinger Bands

Traders use Bollinger Bands to highlight areas of overdone market activity and get a sense for how risky a market is to trade. The indicator is calculated as a chosen number of standard deviations both above and below a simple moving average of the price or exchange rate action over a selected period.

Common parameters include two standard deviations and a 20-period moving average. Traders might use the indicator to buy at the lower band or sell at the higher band. They would then look to close the position when the market moves back to its moving average.

Directional Movement Index or DMI

The DMI measures trend strength over some chosen time period, usually 14 days. The indicator ranges from 0 to 100 and generally comes with three components, the +DI (strength of upward trend), -DI (strength of downward trend) and ADX (Moving Average of the DMI).

When the +DI line crosses upward above the –DI line, a buy signal is generated because the prevailing trend is now upward, according to the indicator.

Momentum Indicator

The Momentum Indicator measures the speed of market changes and is commonly used to identify the strength of market moves. It can also be used on moving averages.

Stochastics Oscillator

The Stochastics Oscillator is a particular type of momentum indicator used to provide a clue to directional changes in the market.

A trade alert arises when the price or exchange rate diverges from the %D line the indicator plots, but the trade signal itself comes when the faster-moving %K line crosses the slower %D line of the indicator.

CHAPTER 3: TRADING WITH TECHNICAL ANALYSIS

Those performing technical analysis for financial assets like stocks, currency pairs or commodities often look at price charts to discern classic patterns, trends and ranges. They might also plot indicators computed from market observables like price, volume and open interest.

Technical analysis for traders can also involve performing a detailed market review that sometimes goes back over years of historical price data in order to determine what sort of cycle the market is in. Such traders may use one of the major market movement theories, like Elliott Wave Theory for example, that can offer considerable predictive power to traders compared to the more standard chart pattern and indicator-based technical analysis methods.

Since so many technical trading methods exist, part of the challenge in performing technical analysis is choosing what patterns to look for and what indicators to use and include in your trade plan. Although the specifics of each popular indicator will be covered in Chapter 5, the following sections will discuss some of the practical aspects of trading in the financial markets using technical analysis.

Using Technical Analysis to Trade

When it comes to using technical analysis to trade financial markets, a wide variety of options are readily available that could suit either the novice or more advanced trader.

Some of the more popular of these technical trading choices appear below in approximate order of the complexity involved in implementing them, as well as some helpful suggestions for using technical analysis to trade financial markets.

Read a Technical Newsletter

Perhaps the easiest way that a novice trader could start using technical analysis to trade would be to start reading a technical analysis newsletter.

This way, they would receive the ongoing directional advice of professional technical analysts. Then, as they read the newsletter over time, they can gradually attempt to replicate the analytical results that the technical pros provided.

Subscribe to a Trade Signal Generating Service

A relatively modern development in trading involves using technical trading signal services. These companies generally provide trade signals based on trade plans developed by experts who offer them to the public as commercial products for either a one-time fee or on an ongoing payment basis.

You can simply subscribe to one of these services by paying their fees, and they will provide you with technical trading signals. Subscribers generally then have the choice as to whether to take the signals or not and about how much to place at risk on each trade.

Educate Yourself about Technical Analysis Methods

In addition to this book, many good books have been written about technical analysis, including John Murphy's classic "Technical Analysis of the Financial Markets."

Also, the Internet hosts plenty of online educational material on a variety of websites about using technical analysis to trade financial markets ranging from relatively obscure indicators to the classic chart patterns.

Furthermore, if you happen to have personal access to an experienced technical analyst, they can probably provide you with some helpful trading tips to get you started on the right foot.

Obtain a Charting Service

For those who want to start doing their own technical analysis, perhaps the most important thing do-it-yourself technical traders need is charting software.

This essential computer program should not only provide up-to-date exchange rates for currency pairs or prices for assets that you will need to analyze, but they should also feature the ability to:

- View high and low points on the chart
- Plot bar and candlestick chart types
- Chart different periods, including hourly, daily and weekly.
- Draw trend lines, channels and horizontal lines.
- Allow chart annotations.
- Superimpose indicators you want to use and read levels.
- Save charts and templates for future reference.

Develop a Successful Technical Trade Plan

By learning from the experience of others, and perhaps also by experimenting with different technical indicators and analysis methods, persistent traders using technical analysis to trade financial markets usually eventually come up with a winning trade plan.

Naturally, your trade plan does not have to win every trade it suggests, provided that it generates bigger winning trades than losing trades over the long term. Back-testing your technical plan over historical exchange rate or price data can help you assess its past success.

Automate Your Technical Trade Plan

As financial markets traders advance in applying their technical analysis skills and develop a successful and objective technical trading plan, many increasingly wish to program or have someone else program a computer to do all of the trading for them so that they can sit back and relax. What was once only a trader's dream has now become possible in reality!

Some novice traders might prefer to use commercial trading robot software for this purpose, but more advanced traders can now either program or have programmed their own personalized automated trading software that can execute deals automatically through many online brokers or exchanges.

Most of the off-the-shelf trading programs you can purchase operate as so-called Expert Advisors using the popular MetaTrader platforms. Nevertheless, custom trading algorithms can also be developed to trade via online brokers using their proprietary Application Programming Interface or API. This refers to the platform or interface that allows your trading platform to connect with the market.

Trading plan automation is an important topic for technical traders and will be covered in greater detail toward the end of Chapter 4 of this book.

Identifying and Trading Ranges

Ranges are one of the most popular and reliable patterns used in technical analysis to forecast future price or exchange rate behavior, and those speculators who seek such patterns out to trade according to a specific plan could be called range traders. This usually short-term trading strategy can be encapsulated with the phrase "buy low and sell high."

Ranging or range-trading markets generally consist of time periods when the market fluctuates between levels of support on the downside and levels of resistance on the upside. When in a trading range, exchange rates or prices tend to move within a tight band and usually exhibit no clear trending tendencies.

When trading ranges occur as part of an overall decline in the market for an asset, this implies that market participants are accumulating or taking in the asset. Conversely, when ranging markets happen during an upwards trend, this indicates that traders are distributing or selling out the asset.

Some of the more common range trading strategies will be covered below in further detail, along with how to go about identifying and trading ranges seen in the financial markets.

Identifying Trading Ranges

A trading range can be identified by drawing parallel horizontal lines between the support area at its base and the resistance area at its top. When the market has confirmed a trading range by making two significant tops at roughly the same level and two significant bottoms at a similar lower level, this will generally allow a trader to identify that a trading range is in progress.

At this point, a more conservative range trader would look to profit from this opportunity by selling as the market rate approaches the top line, and buying as the market approaches the bottom line. Stops on shorts would be placed above the top line, while stops on longs would be placed safely below the bottom line.

Furthermore, from a range trader's perspective, they expect the market to eventually return to trade at the same price or exchange rate within the range irrespective of which direction the market is headed. As a result, a more aggressive range trader might start with an initial trade just to get their feet wet, and then they might add to that position if they see a better level using a "doubling up" or averaging strategy.

While many traders wisely avoid using this strategy, because it can result in excessive losses in trending markets, doubling up has a higher expected return if a trading range has first been established. This fact highlights the importance of assessing market conditions prior to selecting a trading strategy.

Range Trading in Practice

To use a range trading strategy in practice, a trader would first establish a long or short position, even if the market was trading near the center of its trading range.

If the market then went in favor of their position, they would take profits near the range extremities. Nevertheless, if the market went against their position, they might double up the position near the extremities to improve or "average" their rate.

They would then seek to close out the averaged position when the market returned closer to the range center.

Identifying and Trading Trends

Many traders consider trends one of the most popular and reliable price patterns used in technical analysis to forecast future market behavior. Those speculators who seek such patterns out to trade according to a specific plan could be called trend traders.

Financial markets traders often implement this particular trading strategy in medium-term to long-term time frames, and it can be encapsulated by the well-known market aphorism, "The trend is your friend."

The rest of this section discusses how to go about identifying and trading trends seen in the financial markets.

Identifying a Trend

In general, trending markets consist of time periods when the exchange rate moves substantially in one direction or the other. If the directional movement is upwards, the market is said to be in an upwards or up trend. Conversely, when the directional move is downwards, the market is said to be in a downward or down trend.

A trend can be readily identified by reviewing exchange rate charts to look for a series of higher highs and higher lows in the exchange rate to indicate an uptrend. Alternatively, a series of lower highs and lower lows signals a down trend.

Lines known as trend lines can be drawn through these highs and lows to indicate where future support or resistance might lie. When those top and bottom trend lines run parallel, they form a chart pattern called a channel.

Trading Trends

Trend traders often employ a trading method where they initially identify a trend forming in a market once a significant reversal has been seen in its price or exchange rate. Once identified, the trend generally needs to be confirmed before taking a position by using a technical indicator like a set of short-term and longer-term moving averages.

Upon confirmation, trend traders then look for opportunities to enter trades in the direction of that trend on market pull-backs or corrections. Eventually, a position is established in the direction of the trend, and orders will then be placed to liquidate the position, usually at pre-determined take-profit and stop-loss levels.

Furthermore, after taking a trade with the trend, a trader will then seek to ride the trend as far as possible with the position often trailing their stops a certain degree behind the price action to protect existing profits. Eventually, the trend trader will want to close out the position just as the directional move finalizes.

Trend Trading in Practice

In practice, traders often end up liquidating positions once the trend has ended or taken a breather. In order to identify such pauses or reversals in a trend promptly to protect their gains, a trend trader will often follow market movements closely.

They may also use different technical indicators that provide trend reversal signals — like a pair or moving averages, the Moving Average Convergence Divergence or MACD indicator, or the Directional Movement Indicator or DMI — to alert them to a pending trend reversal.

Trend traders might also look to take advantage of market swings within a trend. For example, when trading an upwards move they might look to establish long positions ahead of the rising trend line below the price action and to close these longs ahead of the rising trend line above the price action. The opposite would be the case if trading a down trend.

Swing Trading

Swing trading has proven itself popular as a technical trading strategy among many traders over the years. The financial markets generally lend themselves particularly well to using short-term trading strategies, and so swing trading can suit traders looking to capitalize on moves in that market that last more than one day.

A swing trader typically looks for market moves of shorter duration, and they will tend to hold a position for one to five days, although in some cases they might stay in a trade for several weeks. This contrasts with a day trader who generally will not hold positions overnight. Swing traders often use a number of different market signals and technical indicators to evaluate the optimum entry and exit points in the market.

The rest of this section outlines some of the more popular technical swing trading strategies and compares swing trading to the other trading strategies mentioned in previous sections.

Swing Trading Strategies

The way that most swing traders evaluate the market depends on levels of support and resistance commonly found within a major trend. Such traders generally wait for a market to hit resistance or support levels within the major trend.

They might then initiate a new position or add to an existing one once confirmation of the price direction has been made. After such confirmation, the trader will attempt to initiate the position supported by the momentum of the market's resumed direction.

Another swing trading strategy might involve trading against the major trend in the short-term. Such a trader will watch the market move into either a support or a resistance zone in one direction, and they then will take position that will profit from a correction of the initial move. Stops will usually be placed beyond the identified support or resistance zone.

Traders often find swing trading systems relatively easy to develop. A technical analysis plan based on levels of support and resistance, perhaps combined with two other indicators to confirm the short-term trend, are often all a trader needs. Kept simple, swing trading can be relatively easier to manage than a day trading strategy, for example, but it requires the trader to maintain a disciplined approach.

Swing Trading versus Trend Trading

Swing traders have a somewhat different outlook from the trend traders mentioned in the previous section because they will often look to capitalize on price moves contrary to the major trend. In contrast, trend traders generally look to identify a trend and establish positions on that side of the market to profit from it.

Also, trend traders typically hold their positions for a considerably longer period of time than swing traders. A trend trader will simply identify the major trend and look for opportunities to initiate a position in that direction.

A swing trader, on the other hand, will generally identify a trend and watch as levels of support and resistance become clearly defined. After the swing trader has established levels of support and resistance, a confirmation by another set of indicators is often required before they initiate a trading position.

Swing Trading in Practice

When operating in the market in practice, swing traders typically use indicators like the exponential moving averages or EMA's and/or a certain reading criteria for the Relative Strength Index or RSI to signal that a market is overdone in a particular direction and hence due for a correction. Once the direction has been confirmed by their chosen indicators, the swing trader will then initiate a position to profit from the anticipated move.

As in all good trading plans, swing traders will place stop-loss orders to control risk in the event they were wrong. They may also place an order to liquidate the position in order to take profits at one or more appropriate levels.

Swing Trading versus Range and Trend Trading

Swing trading occupies a grey area between range trading and trend trading, since they could take profitable advantage of either market. Swing trading is also relatively straightforward to perform and could make a good fit for newer traders and seasoned traders alike, as long as they are willing to take positions overnight.

Furthermore, since swing traders make money both from trending moves, counter-trend corrections and ranging markets, the profits they earn by swing trading can even be larger than those earned by trend or range traders. Nevertheless, since swing traders tend to trade more often, the transaction costs they pay can significantly impact their profitability, although less so than with an active day trading or scalping strategy, for example.

Overall, swing trading definitely merits further study and consideration for those prepared to hold trading positions overnight.

Generating Trading Signals

Generating trading signals usually involves performing one or more types of technical analysis. Therefore, the first step in learning how to generate trade signals generally involves learning about the various technical analysis techniques and how they can be applied and combined to create a profitable trading strategy.

Furthermore, a good trading system will not only generate trading signals, but will also give the trader clear indications of where to get in, where to get out profitably and where to admit their trade went wrong and should therefore be closed out for a loss.

Observing price patterns, technical indicators, and support and resistance levels comprise some of the most common ways to generate trading signals, and these techniques each enjoy a wide following.

An explanation and example for each of these useful technical analysis techniques appears below that discuss how experts go about generating trading signals to assist them in trading the financial markets profitably.

Trading Using Price Patterns

Price charts have been used by traders to forecast the future direction of market prices for over a century. When these charts became readily available to financial markets traders, many of them would look for classic chart patterns. These patterns form due to the reflection of the market's mass psychology and supply and demand effects in its observed price levels.

Many of these price patterns have points that — when breached — generate a computable price objective in addition to suggesting a stop level. These points on the chart allow traders to take on positions objectively with clear levels in mind to both take their profits and manage their risk by cutting losses.

This type of signal generation usually requires human interpretation to detect the pattern on the chart in the first place, although computers can now offer considerable assistance in charting the prices, in calculating the likely price objectives and even sometimes in tentatively recognizing classic price patterns.

Trading Using Technical Indicators

A trading system based on technical indicators usually applies a set of criteria whereby, when certain levels are reached, a buy signal, a sell signal or a stay flat signal would be generated.

Perhaps the most popular way of generating trading signals involves using one or more of the technical indicators that will be discussed in detail in Chapter 5. Various market observables are used to determine the value of these indicators, including price, volume and open interest, when applicable.

Some of the popular technical indicators that a trading system might take into account when generating trading signals might include:

- Moving Averages – the price average computed over a set period, for example 5, 10, 30 or even 200 days that then moves forward in time using the same averaging period.

- The Relative Strength Index or RSI – This useful momentum oscillator indicates an overbought market that can be sold over 70 and an oversold market that can be bought under 30.

- Bollinger Bands – This indicator is related to historical volatility and provides two lines situated around the market at a particular standard deviation. Price action nearing the top or bottom of a Bollinger Band can respectively signal a sell or a buy.

The above indicators generate trading signals that comprise some of the more popular in common usage among traders. An in-depth study of the various technical indicators presented in Chapter 5 will provide the trader with additional useful indicators that can generate trading signals.

Trading Support and Resistance Levels

"Buy low and sell high" has often jokingly been considered the prime directive when trading, since doing this is by far easier said than done. Nevertheless, by making a detailed visual study of past price reversal points on a chart, a technical analyst can get a good idea of at what price levels on the chart people would be willing to buy and sell.

For example, the so-called "support levels" below the current market price indicate where traders might have placed purchase orders or simply show buying interest, either to establish long position or to take profits and cover short positions. These levels get their name because they support the market and prevent the market from moving lower.

Conversely, the price levels above the prevailing price where sellers emerge to take profits on long positions or go short the market are commonly known as "resistance levels." They get their name since the price has moved up sufficiently to attract sellers that provide resistance to the market moving higher.

A trading plan could be created to generate forex trading signals based on support and resistance levels. Such a plan might involve buying ahead of key support levels and selling ahead of where the market finds resistance.

Stop-loss orders could be placed comfortably below the support levels and above resistance levels. Orders to take profits could then be placed before the resistance levels and ahead of support levels.

JAY AND JULIE HAWK

CHAPTER 4: TECHNICAL ANALYSIS AND TRADING SOFTWARE

Technical analysis was so much harder and more time consuming to perform before the advent of computers and the ready availability of real time price feeds and historical data.

These days, most traders find themselves in the fortunate position of being able to access technical analysis software that uses live price feeds from exchanges or online brokers.

This rest of this chapter will cover price quotes and historical data feeds, as well as the primary types of technical analysis and trading software that financial markets traders will probably want to make use of.

Trading Software

Online stock trading became available to retail traders online relatively quickly once the Internet started to take off, with early online stockbrokers like E*TRADE gaining a large market share. When it came to servicing the retail sector in the foreign exchange and commodity markets, a variety of software packages have recently become available to trade currency pairs and CFDs with via online brokers.

Furthermore, the number of trading software packages seems to have mushroomed lately, as each of the huge financial markets has gradually found its way online. As a result, more and more personal traders have been attracted to trade these markets as a direct result of their easy accessibility in recent years.

Much of this online trading software strikingly resembles cheap copies of proprietary trading software that banks, financial institutions, fund managers, and other market professionals were paying hundreds of thousands — if not millions — of dollars for their in-house programmers to develop in the 1980's and 90's. These days, some trading software systems can even be downloaded for free online, such as the rather sophisticated MetaTrader 4 and 5 trading platforms developed by MetaQuotes.

The rest of this section discusses different types of trading software, including charting, trading, trading signal generators and news feed software.

The MetaTrader 4 or 5 Trading Platform

As mentioned in the previous section, one of the more useful and comprehensive trading software programs available for download without charge just has to be the MetaTrader 4/5 or MT4/MT5 trading platform that can be used to trade foreign and Contracts for Difference (CFDs) online.

Basically, MT4/5 uses your Internet connection to provide pretty much all of the trading software services you will ever need as a personal trader. Furthermore, if this platform lacks a certain indicator or chart type you prefer, chances are that some bright software programmer has already coded it already and made it available to download so that it can be added to your basic MetaTrader installation.

Besides the MT4/5 software's all-important support for online deal execution and order entry, the additional features of MetaTrader 4 include such useful things as:

- Real time market quotes, price charts and news,
- A variety of popular and customizable technical indicators,
- Support for both live and demo forex trading accounts,
- The proprietary MQL4/5 language for programming Expert Advisors, trade signals, custom indicators and scripts, and
- The ability to automate your trading plans and back-test them to determine what their past success or failure would have been on an extensive free database of historical market data.

Trading Robot Software Can Fully Automate Your Trading

When it comes to time-saving trading software, few packages can compare with the so-called trading robots. Like their name implies, these programs can completely automate the trading process.

Not only does this type of software-based trading robot monitor the market for you around the clock, but it also initiates positions and enters closing orders at pre-determined levels. Even an absolute novice trader, with a very little trading software experience, could figure out how to install one of these trading robots and set it running live trading their margin account while they do other things.

Most of the trading software robots currently on the market operate within MT4/5 as so-called Expert Advisors. This group includes the especially well-known forex trading robots like FAP Turbo and Forex Megadroid.

Nevertheless, if you are a more advanced forex trader, perhaps with some programming experience, you do not have to buy a vendor's automated trading software off the shelf to automate your trading. Fortunately, just about any objective trade plan can now become fully-automated as long as you can execute it via MT4/5 and program it into the platform using the MQL4/5 programming languages.

Additional Trading Software Types

Some software vendors offer packages that provide trading signals, without actually automating trading activity itself. Typically, such signal-generating software monitors the relevant market tirelessly, and then alerts the trader when an opportunity arises. The trader then uses their discretion to decide whether or not to take the advice of their signal generating software.

Other types of software might provide just a portion of the functionality of MetaTrader 4/5, like charting, trading or news services perhaps. Nevertheless, since MT4/5 is currently still being given away for free, that other software presently seems redundant.

Real Time Price Quotes

Thanks in large part to the rise of the Internet, the days of real time price quotes for those who do not work for major financial institutions has now arrived. Anyone with an Internet connection and a computer running a recent operating system can pull up hundreds, if not literally thousands, of websites offering real time quotes on a wide variety of tradable assets, in addition to news wire feeds and even price charts — all often at no cost.

Unless you live in primitive conditions outside the network of the World Wide Web, the old days when you had to chart prices by hand, read the newspaper or call a bank or stockbroker for a real time quote have thankfully gone the way of the dinosaur. In the place of those time-consuming activities, you can now just type the name or code of the asset you wish to get a price for into your Web browser's search engine and then check out all of the tempting real time quotation options.

The rest of this section discusses the types of real time quotes, news feeds and trading opportunities that are currently available to online traders, focusing primarily on the online forex market. Still, most markets can now be traded online by retail traders due to the availability of online Contract for Difference or CFD brokers that offer margin accounts to trade stocks, indexes, commodities and currency pairs.

Real Time Forex Dealing Systems

When it comes to trading currencies, to give you a rough idea of how huge the online forex market has become, as of this writing Google has over 100 million results and Yahoo has over 30 million results for the keyword "forex".

What does all of this mean? Well, forex has basically become a very popular topic among the online community by just about any measure. Perhaps this makes sense since the foreign exchange market is the largest global financial market and boasts a massive average daily transaction volume of over $5 trillion. The forex market also trades around the clock, with especially active Interbank market trading occurring in the major money-center cities of London, New York and Tokyo.

Most of the financial institutions that participate in the Interbank forex market get their real time spot forex quotes from well-established professional market data providers like Reuters Dealing 3000, as well as the more recent Electronic Broking Service or EBS. EBS was also one of the first organizations to allow algorithmic trading in spot foreign exchange via its Application Programming Interface or API.

Nevertheless, to the delight of the growing community of online forex traders, the forex market has recently become one of the very few financial markets that can be traded online in just about any size. Not only are real time forex quotes available online, but freely available online dealing platforms like MetaTrader mean you can trade forex around the clock from anywhere you can get Internet service, including from mobile devices like smartphones.

Automatic Real Time Forex Robots and Trading Platforms

An even more exciting recent development for forex traders, especially those who like to have some free time to spend with their families, has been the invention of online automated forex trading software, or the so-called forex robots as mentioned in the previous section. The majority of these automatic trading programs run as so-called Expert Advisors within the popular MetaTrader 4 or 5 online trading platform that can be downloaded online at no charge.

It seems the future has finally arrived when it comes to getting real time forex quotes, as well as access to timely forex-related news feeds and online forex dealing. If you have an interest in trading forex for your own account and even perhaps fully automating your trading plan, now really is the time to check out what fascinating options have become available online for the personal trader.

If you prefer to trade in other financial markets than the forex market, then you may be interested to discover that many online brokers offer an execution service in CFDs on the most popular stocks, stock indexes and commodities, which makes those assets readily tradable online as well.

Technical Analysis Software

Technical analysis software used to just refer to computer programs that charted market action and allowed traders and technical analysts to draw trend lines and superimpose technical indicators over price action.

Recently, however, the trading software world has been transformed by the development of automated trading software, trade signal generators and custom technical indicators, as well as other sophisticated computer-assisted algorithms for analyzing market movements that include the use of artificial intelligence techniques like machine learning. The recent rise of artificial intelligence has even brought a very complex task like chart pattern recognition that previously could only be performed by humans into the realm of some of the more sophisticated technical analysis software.

The rest of this section describes some of the basic types of technical analysis software and what benefits each of them offer to the technical trader.

Charting Technical Analysis Software

Perhaps the most important technical analysis software for the do-it-yourself technical analyst will be charting software. The program selected for this purpose will need to provide real-time market pricing for each of the assets you want to analyze and probably also needs features like the following:

- Option to plot different chart types include bar and candlestick charts.
- Ability to view rates on charts and indicators by putting your cursor over them.
- Choice of various periodicities including hourly, daily and weekly data.
- Ability to plot trend lines, flat lines, retracement levels and channels over the price action.
- Permit the user to notate charts.
- Include a variety of popular technical indicators.
- Allow for charts and chart templates to be saved for later use.

A popular example of charting software is the MetaTrader 4/5 trading platform that provides all of the aforementioned features for forex traders, as well as the ability to automate trades based on technical signals.

Pattern-Matching Technical Analysis Software

This relatively-recent type of technical analysis software uses advanced pattern-matching algorithms and artificial intelligence to identify traditional and reliable chart patterns.

Some programs even indicate how certain they are about the pattern, as well as what its trigger points and breakout objectives are. Other programs focus on implementing specific technical analysis methods like Elliott Wave Theory, for example.

Trade Signal Generating Software

Now available from a variety of commercial vendors, trade signal generating technical analysis software has become increasingly popular of late.

Although signal generating software generally falls short of actually executing the deals it recommends for you, it usually provides an audible signal along with a trade recommendation, including information like:

- Which currency pair to deal
- In what direction to take the trade
- Where to liquidate the position at a profit
- Where to close the trade out at a loss if the market takes a turn for the worse.

Creating custom indicators and using existing indicators to provide trade signals are some of the sophisticated abilities those using the MetaTrader 4/5 trading platform software have access to.

Automated Trading Software

Perhaps bored by looking at trading screens or disappointed in the profitability of their own trade plans, some traders now choose to use commercial trading robot software to perform their trading thanks to the recent rise of online automated trading.

Basically, you can now purchase an off-the-shelf automatic forex trading robot that comes complete with a built-in expert trade plan that can often be tailored to suit your risk tolerance and have its performance improved by adjusting parameters.

Alternatively, you can have your own software written around a trade plan you have personally developed and implemented for you by an algorithmic trading software expert so that you can trade via a supportive online broker.

Furthermore, if you want to write your own fully automated trading software, then you will first want to set up an account with an online broker or exchange that supports this feature.

In addition, you will need appropriate programming skills, as well as access to advanced trading software that will allow you to back-test your trading plan over historical data and sometimes even optimize parameters for profitability, maximum drawdowns and other trading system performance metrics.

You can usually then trade your plan in a demo or practice account for a reasonable test period before going live on your funded account. Starting out with small sizes when switching to a live account usually also makes sense from a safety perspective before allowing the robot to trade in larger amounts.

Automated Trading Software

Thanks to the development of new technologies like automated trading software, and the availability of retail trading accounts on the Internet, anyone with even a small amount of money to put at risk can now begin trading in the forex, stock or commodity market.

While stocks could be traded by an individual over the telephone via a stockbroker, up until the advent of electronic trading, the forex and commodity markets were only readily accessible to banks, large corporations, high-net worth individuals, fund managers, and those individuals who could fund a margin account with a futures exchange.

Nevertheless, with the advent of the Internet and the subsequent introduction of online trading, the size of the retail trading community has grown exponentially, as the retail market has begun to enter the financial markets in droves.

The following sections discuss popular automated trading software and the advantages it offers for experienced and inexperienced financial markets traders.

Electronic and Automated Trading

Electronic trading has been around for almost thirty years and has its origins in the equities market where open outcry-style stock exchanges have gradually given way to automated trading systems starting in the mid-1980's. The forex market has only started to automate more recently, perhaps because of its global and largely-unregulated nature, not to mention the lack of a centralized marketplace. Online commodity trading via CFDs and futures contracts seems even more recent.

Despite some initial drawbacks for forex and commodity traders, in the past few years, automated trading software has become an increasingly popular way to trade these markets — and for good reason. The main advantage that automated trading programs provide is that the so-called "robot trading" software truly makes trading effortless.

You no longer have to watch any screens, have a background in financial markets trading, do any exhaustive research on economic fundamentals, or even review any technical indicators to initiate a trade. The automatic trading software comes pre-programmed by expert traders and trading system developers to analyse the market using objective and effective technical analysis techniques and optimized parameters.

The trading robot then determines suitable entry and exit points, sizes positions appropriately, and initiates a position automatically, as well as placing liquidation orders to exit the trade for either a profit or loss. All of this is done completely automatically, without you having to lift even a finger. The only thing you have to do is keep your trading account funded if the live trading results do not show the impressive profits found on the trading robot vendor's sales page.

The MetaTrader 4 or 5 Trading Platform

With respect to forex trading platforms, one especially popular option that had been mentioned earlier is MetaTrader 4/5. Also called MT4/5 for short, this platform is offered for online download at no charge by its developer MetaQuotes. In addition to a desktop and web-based version, MT4/5 is also available for use on mobile devices and tablets.

MT4/5 provides the data and trade execution facility for some of the most popular trading robots that have thus far been developed, like the FAP Turbo and Forex Megadroid packages used to trade currency pairs for example.

Not only can you trade in a fully automated manner using an off-the-shelf trading robot with MT4 or 5, but you can even use their proprietary MQL 4/5 programming language to develop your own expert advisor, custom indicator or trade signal generator based on your personal trading plan.

Getting Your Trading Robot Started Trading

Most automated online trading software works as an "Expert Advisor" or EA within a trading platform like MetaTrader 4 or 5 that then interfaces with an online forex broker that holds your margin account.

To get started trading automatically, you will first need just a few minutes to purchase, download and install the trading robot software of your choice in the directory of a compatible trading platform on your computer that allows you access to the markets you wish to trade.

The next important step will be to open and fund a margin trading account with a reputable online broker that offers an execution service in all the specific assets you wish to trade.

Once the funds hit your trading account, you can start your trading robot running. The robot monitors the markets while you watch it or do other things, and it then advises your trading platform to initiate a trade when the market's price action reaches trade points determined by the software based on its trading parameters that are entered into the software ahead of time. The robot also simultaneously places liquidating orders to close any initiated positions out.

At this point, you can just sit back and watch the trading robot's performance as it trades day and night in your account. You might also wish to adjust its parameters to suit your risk tolerance, which many trading robots permit you to do

Programming Your Own Trading Robot

If you have programming experience or the funds to hire a professional programmer, then you can probably learn how to create your own "Expert Advisor". Expert Advisors are basically software programs that operate via the popular MetaTrader 4 and 5 trading platforms.

Furthermore, many institutional traders — as well as those who do not operate on the Windows-based operating systems to which MetaTrader is most suitable — increasingly like to develop their algorithmic trading solutions to work via Algo Terminal.

You can also develop automated trading software that operates using the specific Application Programming Interface or API of the online broker that you intend to use.

Programming Expert Advisors in MetaTrader

One important thing to keep in mind is that the coding language for MetaTrader 4, known as MQL4, is somewhat different from that for

MetaTrader 5, which uses MQL5. Accordingly, so you will need to research how to convert one type of program to the other to make it functional using both MetaTrader platforms. Both languages are similar to C+, so if you already know that programming language, you will be one step ahead of those who do not.

To help you in this software development process, MetaTrader maintains an online database with subroutines that can be included in Expert Advisors, as well as examples of how Expert Advisors are coded. The software's Help files also explain how to edit the EA and set it running in a demo or live account.

Furthermore, once you have written an Expert Advisor that runs in MetaTrader 4 or 5, it is then generally quite simple to use MetaTrader's historical market price data to back test the trading plan programmed into the EA with just a few keystrokes. You can also optimize parameters for the EA based on past performance.

Benefits of Developing Your Own Software

Basically, having the ability to backtest an EA, signal generator or custom indicator and then refine it further via both parameter optimization and additional modifications are some of the great reasons that systematic traders really need to keep in mind when considering automating their trade plans.

If you do not feel comfortable with the risks of doing this programming, testing and optimization yourself, you are invited to contact the authors for a reference to a reputable company with experience programmers that you can hire to do all of that work for you.

The result will be a workable automatic trading robot, signal generator and/or custom indicator, as well as the peace of mind in knowing that your trading system performed adequately well over historical price action to justify you using it in a live trading account.

CHAPTER 5: TECHNICAL INDICATORS EXPLAINED

Technical indicators are computed based upon market observables like price or exchange rate, volume or open interest. Furthermore, computing and using technical indicators involves techniques that can typically be used with any tradable asset. For example, as long as you can obtain the relevant historical market valuation data, you can compute the Relative Strength Index or RSI for a stock, a currency pair or a commodity.

This book has already touched upon some of the more popular technical indicators in Chapter 2. This chapter will add to that information and act as an in-depth reference guide for technical traders to help them gain a better understanding of each of the most popular technical indicators, including how to compute and use them.

Furthermore, when it comes to being successful as a financial markets trader, time is of the essence when making trading decisions based on technical indicators. As a result, you will probably need to create a trading plan based on specific technical indicator signals that will allow you to backtest your system for suitability and trade objectively in a live account.

The following sections of this chapter are intended to be used as reference material for technical analysts interested in learning about the various technical indicators commonly used by those operating professionally in financial markets. The reader will note that each section devoted to the major technical indicators includes for each indicator:

- Its name, history and general description,

- What it measures,
- A sample chart,
- Its common usage among traders, and
- Its term definitions and calculation method.

Also, be aware that this information can change over time, since default indicator parameters can be modified, equations can be enhanced, and new indicators can even be created. Accordingly, while this reference section can certainly be used as a general informational guide to technical indicators, do be sure to review the specifics of each indicator and test calculations thoroughly if you intend to program or have them programmed in an automated system.

Finally, remember to backtest any proposed trading plan over a substantial range of historical data and trading conditions before trading based on any of these indicators and/or their established signals. It is also typically a good idea to test a system by trading it in small amounts in a live account to see how its live performance looks.

The Acceleration/Deceleration or AC Indicator

The Acceleration/Deceleration or AC Indicator was developed by psychologist and trader Bill Williams. It was described and published in his classic book *Trading Chaos* about how to combine trading psychology and Chaos Theory to better understand and forecast market price movements.

The AC indicator shows whether and by how much the momentum of the market (as determined by Bill's Awesome Oscillator) is accelerating or decelerating. The indicator has predictive value for a technical analyst because it changes direction before the momentum, and the momentum changes direction before the market's price. The AC Indicator can therefore provide a useful clue that a directional reversal is forthcoming and can also confirm when a trend seems likely to continue.

The AC indicator histogram fluctuates around zero, where a zero reading indicates that the market's momentum is balanced. A histogram reading greater than zero indicates that the momentum of the market is accelerating, while a level below zero indicates that the market's momentum is decelerating.

Furthermore, the indicator histogram has two colors, usually red and green, that alternate. When the AC value of the current bar is greater than that of the previous bar, it is colored green, and when less than that of the previous bar, it is colored red.

When the indicator changes from green to red above zero, that indicates the acceleration of the momentum is slowing, but still positive. Conversely, when it changes from red to green below zero, that indicates the deceleration of the momentum is slowing, but still negative.

Sample AC Indicator Chart

The AC Indicator is shown in the image below in the indicator box below a bar chart showing the daily exchange rate action for EUR/USD. The chart was obtained from the MetaTrader5 trading platform.

Usage of the AC Indicator

In practice, the Acceleration/Deceleration or AC histogram indicates that you can go ahead and buy when the indicator is colored green or sell when the indicator is colored red. You generally refrain from buying on red or selling on green.

Nevertheless, traders using Bill William's indicators typically ignore any AC signals until they get a Fractal buy or sell signal triggered outside of the Alligator's mouth. Also, they ignore signals in the opposite direction as the first Fractal signal. Finally, if the AC generates a buy or sell signal but the histogram changes color before the order gets executed, they will cancel pending orders.

When trading with the market's momentum (the AC>0 for longs or <0 for shorts), traders look for two green columns to buy or two red columns to sell. For a buy signal, they would put a buy order one tick above the high of the bar corresponding to the second highest high. For a sell signal, they would put a sell order one tick below the low of the bar corresponding to the second lowest low.

Alternatively, if the momentum is contrary to the trade contemplated, (the AC<0 for longs or >0 for shorts) they would need a confirmation in the form of an additional green or red column. Hence, they would require three reds>0 for a short, and three greens<0 for a long when trading against the momentum. Orders would be put one tick beyond the third highest high, for buys, or low for sells.

Calculation Method for the AC Indicator

The AC histogram charts the difference between the Awesome Oscillator or AO and a Simple Moving Average or SMA of the AO taken over five periods. In this case, the AO is calculated as the difference between the 5 and 34 period SMAs of the Median Price observed for those periods.

Definitions:

n	= the number of time periods.
High(n)	= The high price traded during time period n.
Low(n)	= The low price traded during time period n.
SMA(A,B)	= Simple Moving Average of data item A over B periods.
AO(n)	= Awesome Oscillator or momentum for time period n.
AC(n)	= Acceleration/Deceleration Indicator for time period n.

Calculations:

Median Price(n)	= [High(n) + Low(n)] / 2
AO(n)	= SMA[Median Price(n), 5] - SMA(Median Price(n), 34]
AC(n)	= AO(n) - SMA(AO, 5)

The Accumulation/Distribution – A/D Indicator

The Accumulation/Distribution or A/D Indicator was created by Marc

Chaikin and consists of a variation on the more popular On Balance Volume indicator. The A/D Indicator is based on price changes weighted by the trading volume seen when they occur.

The Accumulation/Distribution indicator adds or subtracts the trading volume seen during each period proportionally weighted depending on how that period's close falls between the period's low and high market levels.

In general, when the A/D level increases, that indicates the asset or currency pair is being accumulated or bought since a higher volume trades during upward moves. When the indicator declines, that means the asset is being sold or distributed since volume is higher on downward moves.

Sample A/D Indicator Chart

The A/D Indicator is shown in the image below in the indicator box below a bar chart showing the daily exchange rate action for EUR/USD. The chart was obtained from the MetaTrader5 trading platform.

Usage of the A/D Indicator

When using the Accumulation/Distribution Indicator in practice, traders typically look for divergence between the A/D Indicator and the market exchange rate or price level. When such divergence is seen, it signals a coming directional change in the market.

For example, if the price makes a new significant high within an upwards trend, but the A/D Indicator does not, then it might indicate that the uptrend is losing steam and the market may soon reverse direction. Conversely, if the market makes a fresh low in a down trend, but the A/D Indicators fails to do the same, then that would indicate the down trend might be due for reversal.

The A/D Indicator can also be used to confirm the continuance of a trend when such divergence is absent. In this case, either new lows in the exchange rate prompt new lows in the A/D Indicator to confirm a down trend, or new highs in the rate yield new highs in the indicator to confirm an uptrend.

Calculation Method for the A/D Indicator

A positive or negative weighted volume number is added to the previous value of the A/D indicator to obtain its current value. Generally, if the close is nearer to the high, a more positive weight will be added. If the close is nearer to the low, then a higher negative weight will be deducted from the previous A/D value. Nevertheless, if the close falls exactly in the middle of the high and low prices, then the A/D indicator's value does not change.

Definitions:

n = the number of periods used in the calculation.
High(n) = the highest exchange rate for bar "n".
Low(n) = the lowest exchange rate for bar "n".
Close(n) = the closing exchange rate for bar "n".
Volume(n) = the volume traded during bar "n".
A/D(n) = the Accumulation / Distribution Indicator's value for the current bar "n".
A/D(n-1) = the Accumulation / Distribution Indicator's value for the previous bar "n-1".

Calculations:

A/D(n) =
((Close(n) - Low(n)) - (High(n) – Close(n)))*Volume(n)/(High(n) – Low(n))+ A/D(n-1)

The Alligator Indicator

The Alligator Indicator was initially developed by psychologist and technical trader Bill Williams which he wrote about in his *New Trading Dimensions* book. This sophisticated indicator uses a combination of Smoothed Moving Averages or SMMAs parameterized using fractal geometry and non-linear dynamics.

Bill Williams estimated that trends only occur between 15 to 30% of the time, and yet following them can make traders the most money. Accordingly, Williams used the Alligator Indicator to recognize times when it would be advantageous to follow the trend. He was also able to use it to identify ranging or non-trending markets when it made sense to refrain from trading.

The Alligator Indicator finds its most common usage in identifying trending and ranging markets. In terms of its interpretation, an analogy to an alligator is often used, thereby giving it its name.

The indicator itself consists of three lines, typically colored Blue, Red and Green, which are usually named as follows:

- **Alligator's Jaw:** This blue line is the primary Balance Line and consists of a SMMA that pertains to the time period used in the indicator's construction. It typically consists of a 13-period SMMA, moved forward 8 bars.

- **Alligator's Teeth:** This red line is the Balance Line for the time period one level shorter. It typically consists of an 8-period SMMA, moved forward 5 bars.

- **Alligator's Lips:** This green line is the Balance Line for the time period two levels shorter. It typically consists of a 5-period SMMA, moved forward 3 bars.

The above parts of the Alligator Indicator graphically demonstrate the ongoing interplay of different time frames as they operate in the market.

Sample Chart for the Alligator Indicator

The Alligator Indicator is shown in the image below in the indicator box superimposed over a bar chart showing the daily exchange rate action for EUR/USD. The chart was obtained from the MetaTrader5 trading platform.

Usage of the Alligator Indicator

When traders use the Alligator Indicator to identify trending and ranging markets, an alligator analogy is commonly employed for illustration purposes. Basically, when all of the mythological alligator's parts or Balance Lines converge and are plotted close to one another, that means the alligator is sleeping or nearly asleep and his mouth is closed. This signals that a ranging market prevails.

Nevertheless, the more the creature sleeps, the hungrier it gets, and the first thing it does upon waking is yawn. Then it smells a bull or a bear, and starts to hunt its prey as the indicator's Balance Lines begin to separate and his mouth opens.

An uptrend is indicated if the price trades above the alligator's mouth which consists of its jaw, teeth and lips - the blue, red and green lines respectively. These lines should also be aligned, inclining upwards, with the green over the red over the blue, and all under the price.

Conversely, a downtrend is indicated when the price trades below the alligator's mouth. In this case, the lines should also be aligned, but heading downwards, with the blue line above the red, which is above the green, and all come in over the price.

Once the alligator has killed and eaten sufficiently, it begins to lose interest and fall asleep again, prompting the blue, red and green Balance Lines to converge and cross over as its mouth closes. This indicates the time to take profits has arrived and the trend is over.

Calculation Method for the Alligator Indicator

The Alligator Indicator consists of three lines superimposed over the price chart. The definitions of the inputs and equations used in its calculation are listed below.

Definitions:

n	= The number of time periods.
High(n)	= The high price traded during time period n.
Low(n)	= The low price traded during time period n.
SMMA(A,B,C)	= a Smoothed Moving Average where A refers to the data being smoothed, B refers to the period to be smoothed, and C represents the time period shift.

Calculations:

Median Price(n) = [High(n) + Low(n)] / 2

Alligator's Jaw (Blue Line) = SMMA (Median Price(n), 13, 8)

Alligator's Teeth (Red Line) = SMMA (Median Price(n), 8, 5)

Alligator's Lips (Green Line) = SMMA (Median Price(n), 5, 3)

The Average Directional Index or ADX Indicator

The Average Directional Index or ADX was originally developed by J. Welles Wilder who wrote about it in his book: *"New Concepts in Technical Trading Systems."* This popular technical indicator helps traders determine if a trend exists and if so, how strong it is and in what direction it is heading.

The ADX indicator is most commonly run over a 14 period time frame and consists of the following three lines used in combination:

1. **The Positive Directional Indicator or +DI:** This line represents the strength of the upwards trend.

2. **The Negative Directional Indicator or -DI:** This line indicates the strength of the downwards trend.
3. **The Average Directional Index or ADX:** An average involving the +DI and the –DI levels computed over the 14 period time frame.

Trading signals are generated using the ADX based on crossovers among the +DI and –DI lines and their direction. The ADX is a lagging indicator relative to the price and ranges between 0 and 100. ADX levels under 20 tend to indicate a weak trend, while levels over 40 indicate a strong trend.

Sample Chart of the ADX Indicator

The ADX Indicator is shown in the image below in the indicator box below a bar chart showing the daily exchange rate action for EUR/USD. The chart was obtained from the MetaTrader5 trading platform.

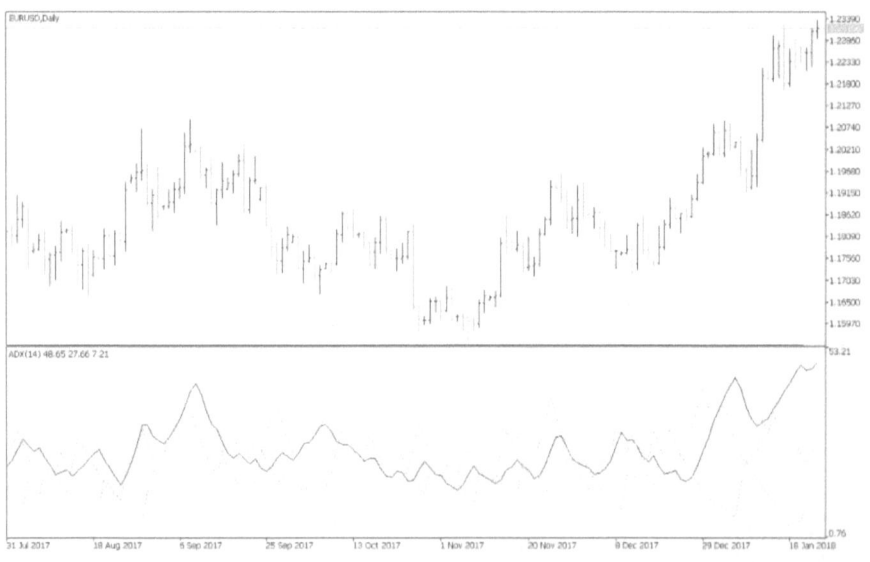

Usage of the ADX Indicator

Traders often observe several things about the Average Directional Movement indicator when using it in practice. First, they will see whether +DI or –DI is on top. An uptrend is indicated by +DI being in the superior position, while a downtrend is indicated by –DI being plotted higher.

Then, traders using the ADX will observe the magnitude of any separation between –DI and +DI. The size of their deviation will indicate the strength of the trend in progress, if any.

When using the ADX to generate trading signals, perhaps the simplest method involves looking for crossover points between +DI and –DI. For example, if –DI crosses upwards above –DI, then a sell signal would be generated as the market turns downward. Alternatively, if +DI crosses above –DI, then a buy signal would be indicated as an uptrend starts to take over.

Some traders add greater complexity to these simple signals by increasing the divergence criteria for a trend to exist and a position to be established. Wilder, on the other hand, suggested using "points of extremeum" that were the high for an uptrend crossover day and the low for a crossover day indicating a downtrend. Once the market price exceeded those points, the signal to trade in the direction of the indicated trend would be triggered.

Calculation Method for the ADX Indicator

The calculation method illustrated below can be varied by using different time periods or by substituting several alternative types of moving averages that might include: simple, weighted and adaptive moving averages, for the exponential moving averages.

Definitions:

n	= the number of time periods.
High(n)	= The high price traded during time period n.
High(n-1)	= The high price traded during the time period immediately prior to n.
Low(n)	= The low price traded during time period n.
Low(n-1)	= The low price traded during the time period immediately prior to n.
Close(n)	= The closing price of time period n.
Close(n-1)	= The closing price of the time period immediately prior to n.
EMA(A,B)	= An Exponential Moving Average of data item A over B periods.
ADX(n)	= The Average Directional Index over n periods.
ATR	= Average True Range, an EMA of the true ranges.

Calculations:

UpMove = High(n) − High(n-1)
DownMove = Low(n-1) − Low(n)

+DM =UpMove if UpMove>0 and >DownMove, otherwise +DM=0

-DM =DownMove if DownMove>0 and >UpMove, otherwise +DM=0

+DI = 100*EMA(+DM/ATR, 14)
This line represents the strength of the upwards trend.

-DI = 100*EMA(-DM/ATR, 14)
This line indicates the strength of the down trend.

ADX(14) = 100 * EMA(ABS(+DI- -DI)/(+DI + -DI), 14)

The Average True Range or ATR Indicator

The Average True Range or ATR indicator give a trader a sense of the volatility or level of price swings prevailing in the market. The indicator was developed by J. Wells Wilder who wrote about it in his "*New Concepts in Technical Trading Systems*" book.

Many successful trading systems use this popular indicator to provide a sense of trading risk that can be useful when sizing positions using risk-based criteria.

A low ATR value of the indicator signals a peaceful, ranging market, while a high ATR value indicates a greater incidence of sharp price swings, or perhaps a dramatic crash or spike in market prices.

Sample Chart of the ATR Indicator

The ATR Indicator is shown in the image below in the indicator box below a bar chart showing the daily exchange rate action for EUR/USD. The chart was obtained from the MetaTrader5 trading platform.

Usage of the ATR Indicator

Traders often use the Average True Range indicator like other volatility indicators to provide a sense of the risk prevailing in the market.

For example, they might use it to weight positions, with a higher ATR value implying that the trader takes a smaller trading position in order to maintain a consistent level of risk among positions taken in different markets or currency pairs. Conversely, a lower ATR value would indicate taking a larger trading position.

In terms of forecasting, the ATR might be used to indicate the chances of a trend reversal. If the ATR value is high, that could indicate a greater probability of a directional change that often comes after a period of high volatility. On the other hand, if the ATR was low, that would tend to indicate a weak trend and a ranging market.

Calculation Method for the ATR Indicator

In essence, the Average True Range is a moving average of the True Range and is usually taken over 14 time periods. Some traders vary the type of moving average used to achieve different goals, perhaps using exponential, smoothed or weighted moving averages instead of a simple average.

Definitions:

n	= the current time period
High(n)	= The high price traded during time period n.
Low(n)	= The low price traded during time period n.
Close(n-1)	= The closing price of the time period immediately prior to n.
SMA(A,B)	= Simple Moving Average of data item A, taken over B time periods.
TR(n)	= True Range for time period n.
ATR(n, B)	= Average True Range taken over B time periods for time period n.

Calculations:

True Range or TR(n) = MAX [{High(n) – Low(n)}, {Close(n-1) - High(n)}, {Close(n-1) - Low(n)}]

ATR(n, 14) = SMA(TR(n), 14)

The Awesome Oscillator Indicator

The Awesome Oscillator or AO was developed by psychologist and trader Bill Williams who described it in his book *New Trading Dimensions*. This trading classic covers how to combine trading psychology and Chaos Theory to better understand and forecast market price movements.

The Awesome Oscillator measures market momentum. Its calculation involves determining the moving average of the median bar price over the last five bars of a chart and then subtracting that from the moving average of the median bar price taken over the last 34 bars.

The AO is usually plotted as a histogram in which bars higher than the preceding bar will be colored green. Bars lower than the preceding one will be colored red.

Furthermore, Bill Williams recommended that the Awesome Oscillator be used in conjunction with his Fractals and Alligator indicators. Specifically, the AO only comes into play once an initial Fractal signal gets triggered outside of the Alligator's "mouth."

Once that criterion is met, the AO can then generate a number of useful trading signals that include Saucer and Twin Peaks buy and sell signals, in addition to crossover signals when the histogram moves over the indicator's key zero line.

Sample Chart of the Awesome Oscillator Indicator

The AO Indicator is shown in the image below in the indicator box below a bar chart showing the daily exchange rate action for EUR/USD. The chart was obtained from the MetaTrader5 trading platform.

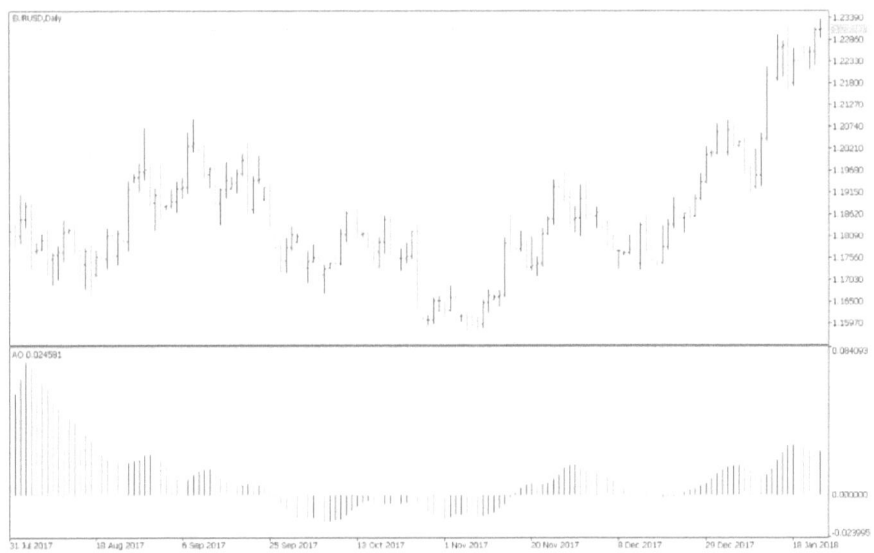

Usage of the Awesome Oscillator

The Awesome Oscillator has several reliable buy and sell signals that it generates, and the general trading rule with the AO involves not buying when the histogram is red and not selling when it is green.

The Awesome Oscillator generates a so-called "Saucer" buy signal when a histogram above the zero point changes direction from down to up. The signal involves three successive bars, the A, B and C bars. The A bar can be of any color, but should be higher than B which needs to be red. The following C bar must be green to generate the signal. Traders using this signal would then enter a buy order one tick above the high of the price bar corresponding to C.

The Awesome Oscillator generals a "Saucer" sell signal when the histogram that is below the zero point changes direction from up to down. The A bar can be of any color, but needs to be lower than B which must be green. The C bar must be red to generate the signal. Traders using this signal would then enter a sell order one tick lower than the low of the price bar corresponding to C.

A Cross signal is generated by the Awesome Oscillator when the histogram crosses the zero point line from below for a buy signal or from above for a sell signal. Traders noting a buy signal would put a buy order one tick above the high of the price bar corresponding to the first bar which crosses the zero point. A sell signal would generate a sell order one tick below the low of the price bar corresponding to the first bar which crosses the zero point. Signal bars are green for buy signals, red for sell signals.

Finally, the Awesome Oscillator generates a "Twin Peaks" buy signal when the histogram is lower than the zero point, and the last bar's low is higher than the previous bar. The histogram cannot be higher than zero in between these two bottoms, and this is the only buy signal generated below zero. Traders would put a buy order one tick above the top of the signal bar, which should be green.

The sell signal occurs when the histogram is higher than the zero point, and the last bar's low is lower than the previous one. Between these two tops, the histogram can never be lower than zero, and this is the only sell signal generated above zero. Traders would put a sell order one tick below the bottom of the signal bar, which should be red.

Calculation Method for the Awesome Oscillator

The Awesome Oscillator Indicator shows current market momentum by computing a 34-period simple moving average and subtracting a 5-period simple moving average from it. Each of the moving averages is determined based on the bar midpoints or median prices.

Definitions:

n	= the number of the time period bar in question.
High(n)	= The high price traded during time period n.
Low(n)	= The low price traded during time period n.
SMA(A,B)	= Simple Moving Average of data item A over B periods.
MP(n)	= Median Price at time period n.
AO(n)	= Awesome Oscillator or momentum at time period n

Calculations:

MP(n) = [High(n) + Low(n)] / 2

Awesome Oscillator or AO(n) = SMA(MP(n), 5) - SMA(MP(n), 34)

Bollinger Bands

The Bollinger Bands are an indicator invented by John Bollinger in the 1980's that evolved out of the idea of trading bands. In practice, Bollinger Bands are used to assess the highness or lowness of a market price relative to where it has previously traded.

The main advantage of Bollinger Bands as a trading indicator involves the fact that they adjust to volatility conditions, which vary with the level of price swings seen over time. As a result, Bollinger Bands generally widen when the market experiences highly volatile periods and narrow during calmer trading periods.

Bollinger Bands are plotted a certain number of standard deviations away from a central moving average, which means they incorporate a measure of market volatility. This contrasts with Envelopes, which are drawn a fixed percentage difference away from an average.

Bollinger Bands will typically be plotted over the price action itself, although some traders prefer to put them underneath the price chart as an indicator. All-in-all, they have become one of the more popular technical indicators since they offer a variety of useful information that traders can use to profit from.

Sample Chart of Bollinger Bands

The Bollinger Bands Indicator is shown in the image below in the indicator box superimposed over a bar chart showing the daily exchange rate action for EUR/USD. The chart was obtained from the MetaTrader5 trading platform.

Usage of Bollinger Bands

Traders generally use Bollinger Bands as trading guides that theoretically should contain most market price swings between the upper line and the lower line of the indicator. This spread widens in more volatile markets, where large price swings become more likely, and narrows in calmer markets. Also, when a price movement initiates from one side of the band, it usually extends to reach the opposite side. This can be used to set price objectives when trading.

A simple trading strategy using Bollinger Bands might involve selling when the market is above the upper line and buying when it is below. That idea can be further refined to only signal trades in the direction of the trend. In this case, you would use Bollinger Bands to signal a short when the central average is sloping downwards and the market is trading above its upper band. Conversely, a long might be signaled when the central average slopes upward and the market is trading below its lower band.

In addition, Bollinger Bands provide several other useful trading signals. For example, when the band has contracted substantially due to low price volatility, this may be an indication that the market may subsequently break out and move sharply in either direction. Furthermore, if the price exceeds the upper line, this tends to indicate the current trend should continue. Alternatively, peaks and dips outside the band followed by peaks and dips inside the band, might indicate a trend reversal.

Calculation Method for Bollinger Bands

In general, Bollinger Bands are characterized by two outer lines, drawn in an equidistant fashion around a middle line that usually takes the form of some type of moving average. The most common Bollinger Band parameters involve using a 20-period Simple Moving Average for the middle line, with the top and bottom lines placed two standard deviations away.

Definitions:

n	= the number of time periods.
Close(n)	= The closing price of time period n.
SMA(A,B)	= A Simple Moving Average of data item A over B periods.
SD(n)	= Standard Deviation as of time period n.
ML(n)	= Middle Line as of time period n.
TL(n)	= Top Line as of time period n.
BL(n)	= Bottom Line as of time period n.
D	= Number of Standard Deviations that TL and BL lie away from ML.
SQRT(A)	= Square Root of A
SUM(1,n,A)	= Sum of A(i) from i=1 to i=n

Calculations:

Standard Deviation or SD(n) = SQRT{SUM[1,n,Close(i)-SMA(Close(i))^2]/n}

Middle Line or ML(n) = SMA(Close, n) = SUM[1,n,Close(i)]/n

Top Line or TL(n) = ML(n) + D*SD(n)

Bottom Line or BL(n) = ML(n) - D*SD(n)

The Commodity Channel Index or CCI Indicator

The Commodity Channel Index or CCI technical indicator was originally published by Donald Lambert in a Commodities Magazine article. The oscillator indicator was originally designed to help traders identify cyclical trends in commodities, but it also has applicability to currency and stock market trading.

Traders typically use the CCI to determine overbought and oversold levels. In addition to that common usage of the oscillator, they might also use price/indicator divergence and trend breaks seen on the CCI graph to generate trading signals.

Sample Chart of the CCI Indicator

The CCI Indicator is shown in the image below in the indicator box below a bar chart showing the daily exchange rate action for EUR/USD. The chart was obtained from the MetaTrader5 trading platform.

Usage of the CCI Indicator

The Commodity Channel Index can generate a variety of buy and sell signals as follows.

- *Overdone Levels:* Traders sometimes use the CCI to show where the market has become oversold or overbought, and hence might be due for correction. Oversold levels generally fall below -100, while overbought levels exceed +100. A trading signal to go long could result from a move from oversold CCI levels to back over -100. While a short trade might be signaled by the CCI returning below +100 after being in overbought territory.

- *Trend Breaks:* Traders often draw trend lines on the CCI chart between peaks or dips and then look for breaks to generate signals. When the CCI is oversold below -100, and has broken above a downward-sloping trend line, then that would give a bullish signal. Similarly, when the CCI is overbought above +100, and has broken below an upward-sloping trend line, then that would give a bearish signal.

- *Divergence:* When the CCI shows positive or bullish divergence relative to the market price in oversold territory under -100, then that would generate a bullish signal when the CCI moves back above -100. Negative or bearish divergence seen in the CCI when overbought above +100 would generate a bearish signal when the CCI falls back below +100.

Calculation Method of the CCI Indicator

The CCI Indicator is an unbounded indicator that is characterized by a single line that oscillates around the zero level, and levels beyond +100 or -100 are considered extreme. The definitions of the inputs and equations used in its calculation are listed below.

Definitions:

n	= the number of the time period bar in question.
N	= the number of time periods in the averaging process.
High(n)	= The high price traded during time period n.
Low(n)	= The low price traded during time period n.
Close(n)	= The closing price at the end of time period n.
TPX(n)	= Typical Price of time period n.
SMA(A,B)	= Simple Moving Average of data item A over B periods.
ABS(A)	= The Absolute Value of data item A.
DEV(n)	= The Deviation of the price from its mean at time n.
CCI(n)	= The Commodity Channel Index value at time period n.

Calculations:

$$TPX(n) = [High(n)+Low(n)+Close(n)]/3$$

$$DEV(n) = ABS[TPX(n) - SMA(TPX(n), N)]$$

$$SMA(DEV(n), N) = SUM[DEV(n), N]/N$$

$$CCI(n) = (1/0.015) * [TPX(n) - SMA(TPX(n),N)]/ SMA(DEV(n), N)$$

Envelopes

The Envelopes technical indicator is formed by using two moving averages where one of them is shifted up by a certain percentage or amount, and the other is shifted down by that same amount or percent. This forms a pair of parallel lines that usually surrounds the price action when suitable parameters are chosen for the indicator.

When choosing Envelope indicator parameters, traders tend to use wider bands with markets that generally have a higher volatility level, and narrower bands with lower volatility markets. Also, Envelopes can either be centered on the price action itself, or on another moving average. The moving averages chosen for the Envelope can also vary, with simple, exponential and weighted moving averages all in common usage.

The idea behind using Envelopes to trade stems from the observation that markets tend to trade to extremes as enthusiastic buyers or sellers fail to see the signs of a price reversal. The market often subsequently corrects to more sustainable levels. Like the Bollinger Band Indicator, Envelopes can provide traders with a sense of when the market may be due for correction.

Sample Chart with Envelopes

The Envelopes Indicator is shown in the image below superimposed over a bar chart showing the daily exchange rate action for EUR/USD. The chart was obtained from the MetaTrader5 trading platform.

TECHNICAL ANALYSIS FOR FINANCIAL MARKETS TRADERS

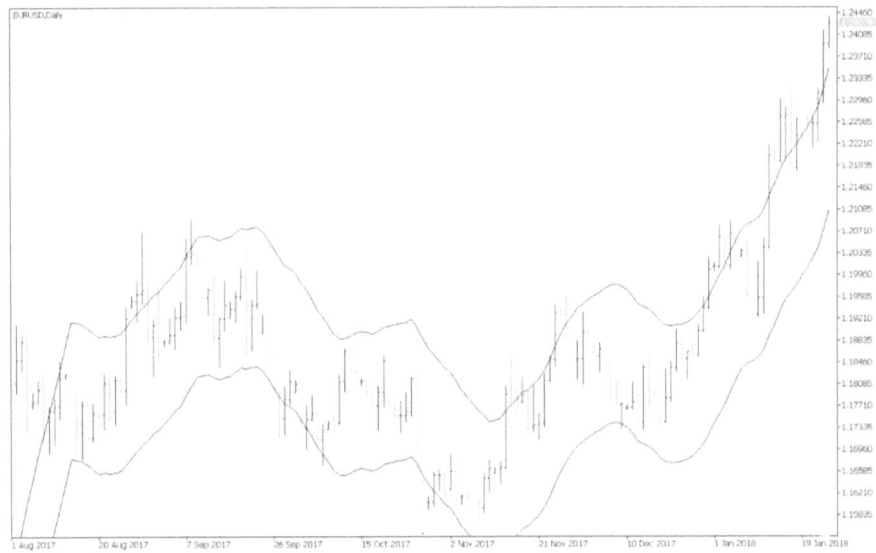

Usage of Envelopes

In general, Envelopes act like the Bollinger Band indicator in that they give theoretical upper and lower boundaries for the market price action to trade between.

The Envelopes indicator generates a sell signal when the market reaches the Upper Envelope line. Conversely, a buy signal is generated when the market touches the Lower Envelope line.

Calculation Method for Envelopes

Envelopes consist of an upper and lower line superimposed over the price chart that generally contain the price action. The definitions of the inputs and equations used in its calculation are listed below.

Definitions:

n	= the number of the time period bar in question.
N	= the number of periods in the smoothing average.
Close(n)	= The closing price at the end of time period n.
K	= The Value of the shift in basis points.
SMA(A,B)	= Simple Moving Average of data item A over B periods.

Calculations:

Upper Envelope = SMA(Close(n), N)*[1+K/1000]

Lower Envelope = SMA(Close(n), N)*[1-K/1000]

The Force Index Indicator

The Force Index technical indicator was originated by Dr Alexander Elder. He published detailed rules for calculating and using this indicator in his book *Trading for a Living*.

In general, the force behind each price movement can be characterized by a direction, a movement size and a volume level. This force will be positive if the current bar's close is above that of the previous bar. If it is lower, then the force has a negative sign.

Basically, the larger the movement from close to close, the higher the market's force is. Also, the force also increases with higher trading volume.

Furthermore, since the Force Index tends to swing considerably, traders often smooth out the data using a moving average that can be a simple, weighted or exponential moving average of the closing prices.

A common technique involves using 2 and 13-day exponential moving average to assess the strength of the short and medium-term trends respectively.

Sample Chart with the Force Index Indicator

The Force Index Indicator is shown in the image below in the indicator box below a bar chart showing the daily exchange rate action for EUR/USD. The chart was obtained from the MetaTrader5 trading platform.

Usage of the Force Index Indicator

In practice, the Force Index helps traders gauge the strength and direction of the prevailing trend. For example, some traders use the slope of the 13-day EMA Force Index to indicate the direction of the trend.

Furthermore, when the Force Index is greater than zero, that indicates the trend is upwards, and when below zero, the trend is downwards. Nevertheless, when the Force Index trades undecidedly around its zero point, this indicates a lack of trend in the market.

In terms of trading signals, traders might use the indicator to go long when the Force Index was under zero and bullish divergence appeared relative to the price. This means that the price makes new lows, but the Force Index fails to do so.

Conversely, traders might go short when the Force Index was over zero and bearish divergence appeared relative to the price. This means that the price makes new highs, but the Index fails to do so.

Calculation Method for the Force Index

The Force Index consists of a single line that fluctuates around zero without having a fixed boundary on either side. The definitions of the inputs and equations used in its calculation are listed below.

Definitions:

n = the number of the time period bar in question.
N = the period of the smoothing using a moving average.
Close(n) = The closing price at the end of time period n.
Volume(n) = The volume traded during time period n.
SMA(A,B) = Simple Moving Average of data item A over B periods.
Forex Index (n) = The value of the Forex Index Indicator at time period n.

Calculations:

Basic Force Index
Force Index(n) = [Close(n) − Close(n-1)] * Volume(n)

Simple Smoothed Force Index
Force Index(n) = [SMA(Close(n), N) − SMA(Close(n-1), N)] * Volume(n)

The Fractals Indicator

The Fractals technical indicator was developed by psychologist and trader Bill Williams who described it in his book *Trading Chaos*. This trading classic covers how to combine trading psychology and Chaos Theory to better understand and forecast market price movements.

Fractals can be either bullish or bearish and consist of recurring price patterns which can be used to confirm price trend reversals. They need to consist of at least five bars, and are typically plotted as a set of high and low arrows superimposed over the reversal points in the price action.

The basic guidelines for identifying a fractal are:

- **Bearish** – when a price pattern has a highest high in the center, flanked by two lower highs.

- **Bullish** – when a price pattern has a lowest low in the center, flanked by two higher lows.

Fractals are lagging indicators so they do not have predicative value for the price since they follow it. Traders generally use them with other indicators to confirm that reversals have indeed occurred.

Sample Chart of the Fractals Indicator

The Fractals Indicator is shown in the image below as arrows superimposed over a bar chart showing the daily exchange rate action for EUR/USD. The chart was obtained from the MetaTrader5 trading platform.

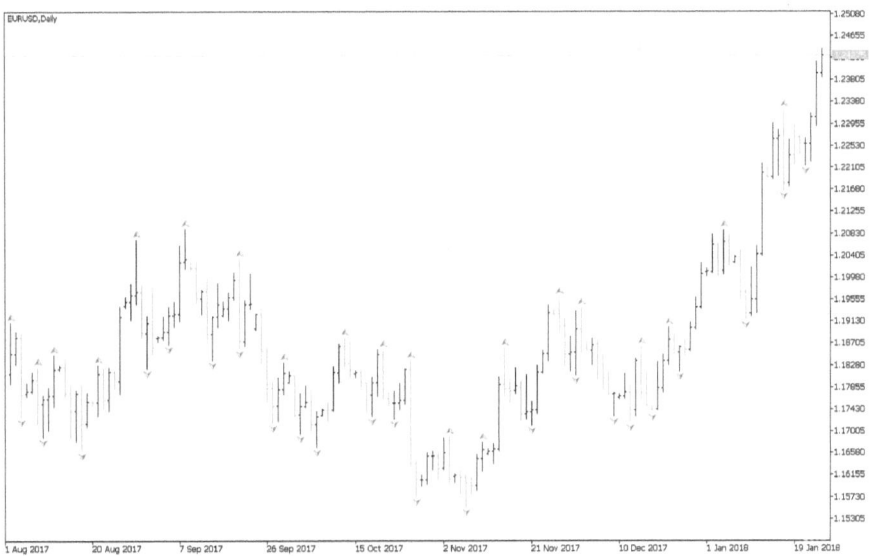

Usage of the Fractals Indicator

Fractals are generally used in identifying whether or not a price reversal has occurred. While not often used on their own, one of the most common usages of Fractals as an indicator is in combination with the Alligator trading system developed by Bill Williams.

For example, a combination trading rule might involve not closing longs or selling if the Fractal is lower than the Alligator's Teeth (the central average or Red Balance Line in the Alligator Indicator). Similarly, you would not close shorts or buy if the fractal is above the Alligator's Teeth.

Furthermore, Bill Williams, in his book *Trading Chaos*, suggested the following trading rules using the Fractal indicator that helps to reduce unprofitable trades:

"Our first signal entry into any market is always the first fractal outside the Alligator's mouth. Once this signal is hit, we will take any and all signals that are triggered in that direction.

If the buy signal is above the Red Balance Line (the Alligator's Teeth), we would place a buy stop one tick above the high of the up fractal. If the sell signal is below the Red Balance Line, we would place a sell stop one tick below the low of the fractal sell signal.

We would not take a fractal sell signal if, at the time it is hit, the price is above the Red Balance Line."

Calculation Method for the Fractal Indicator

The Fractals Indicator consists of red up or down arrows superimposed over the price action signifying when a trade should be taken and in what direction. The definitions of the inputs and equations used in its calculation are listed below.

Definitions:

n   = the number of the time period bar in question.
High(n)   = The high price traded during time period n.
Low(n)   = The low price traded during time period n.

Calculations:

An UP Fractal exists at n if the following conditions are met:
High(n-2) < High(n)
High(n-1) < High(n)
High(n + 1) < High(n)
High(n + 2) < High(n)

A DOWN Fractal exists at n if the following conditions are met:
Low(n-2) > Low(n)
Low(n-1) > Low(n)
Low(n + 1) > Low(n)
Low(n + 2) > Low(n)

The Ichimoku Kinko Hyo Indicator

The name of the Ichimoku Kinko Hyo or IKH indicator means "chart equilibrium at a glance." This very useful technical analysis technique was originated by Tokyo journalist Goichi Hosod in pre-WWII Japan, but was only released to the public in the late 1960's.

In general, the Ichimoku Kinko Hyo indicator provides a wealth of helpful directional information for traders, including clear trading signals. Traders also use the IKH to assess the existence and direction of a trend, as well as to provide initial and secondary support and resistance levels.

The IKH indicator seems to work best on daily or weekly charts, and it consists of five lines that have Japanese names and traditional colors as follows:

1. The The Tenkan-Sen or conversion line is plotted in red.

2. The Kijun-Sen or base line is plotted in maroon.

3. The Chikou Span or lagging span is plotted in pink.

4. The Senkou Span A is plotted in green

5. The Senkou Span B is plotted in blue.

The Senkou Span consists of the shaded area between the Senkou Span A and B lines, while the Ichimoku Cloud or Kumo is the distance between the A and B lines at any given time period.

Sample Chart of the Ichimoku Kinko Hyo Indicator

The IKH Indicator is shown in the image below superimposed over a bar chart showing the daily exchange rate action for EUR/USD. The chart was obtained from the MetaTrader5 trading platform.

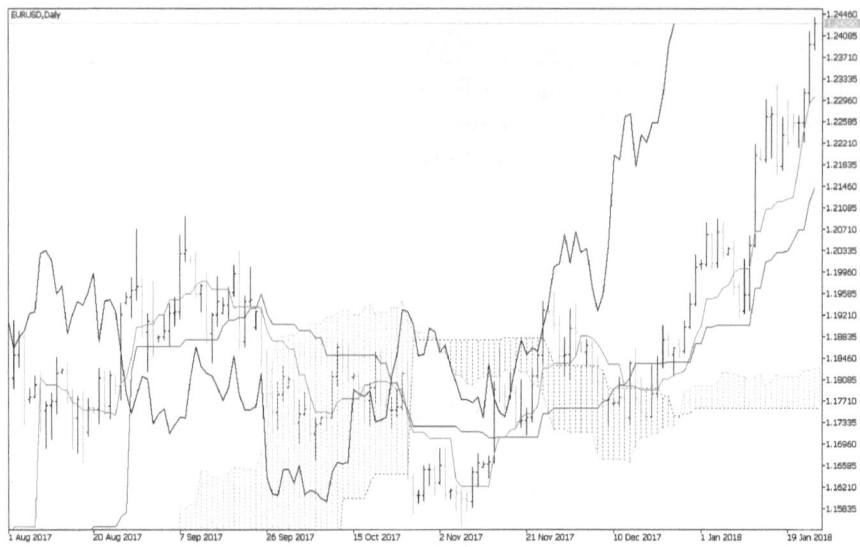

Usage of the Ichimoku Kinko Hyo Indicator

The Tenkan-Sen line indicates the market's trend. If it is rising or falling, the trend exists, but when it is flat, the market is ranging.

The Kijun-sen base line indicates market movement. When the market trades above this line, it will probably continue to rise, and when below it, to fall. When the market crosses the line, a trend reversal becomes likely.

The Kijun-sen and Tenkan-Sen lines can also provide trading signals. When the Tenkan-sen line crosses the Kijun-sen line from below, that generates a buy signal. When it does so from above, that gives a sell signal.

If the Chinkou Span or lagging line crosses upwards above the market price, then that generates a buy signal. Conversely, a short signal occurs if that line crosses below the market price from above.

The vertical line between the Senkou A and B lines is refered to as an Ichimoku Cloud or Kumo. This line provides another trend indicator, and when the price trades below it, that indicates a bearish market, while above it indicates a bullish trend.

Furthermore, when the market trades between lines A and B, the market is not considered to be in a trending state, and support and resistance levels exist at lines A and B. Also, when the market trades over the Ichimoku Cloud, its upper line gives primary support, and its lower line gives secondary support. Conversely, when the market trades under the cloud, the lower line presents primary resistance, and the upper line secondary resistance.

Calculation Method for the Ichimoku Kinko Hyo Indicator

The Ichimoku Kinko Hyo Indicator consists of a fives lines that are superimposed over the price chart. The definitions of the inputs and equations used in its calculation are listed below.

Definitions:

High(n periods) = The high price traded during n time periods.
Low(n periods) = The low price traded during n time periods.
N1 = First number of periods or interval.
N2 = Second number of periods or interval.
N3 = Third number of periods or interval.
N4 = Fourth number of periods or interval.

Calculations:

Tenkan-Sen = [MAX(High(N1 periods) + MIN(Low(N1 periods)]/2

Kijun-Sen = [MAX(High(N2 periods) + MIN(Low(N2 periods)]/2

Chikou Span = The current close price graphed N2 time period bars back.

Senkou Span A = [Tenkan-Sen + Kijun-Sen]/2 and it is graphed N3 time period bars ahead.

Senkou Span B = [MAX(High(N4 periods) + MIN(Low(N4 Periods)]/2 and it is graphed N2 time period bars ahead.

Typical parameters for this indicator might be: N1=8, N2=22, N3=26 and N4=44 time periods.

The Moving Average Convergence/Divergence or MACD Indicator

The Moving Average Convergence/Divergence or MACD indicator is one of the simplest and most reliable momentum indicators available and was initially developed by Gerald Appel. The MACD provides technical analysts with a useful way to determine whether a trend exists, how strong it is, in what direction it is moving and whether it may soon be reversing.

The MACD indicator basically computes the difference between two moving averages of the market price and is often plotted as a histogram of these differences for each time period. The MACD oscillates above and below the zero line and does not have any absolute limits on its value. It can be applied to charts of any time frame.

Typically, traders will use a 26-period and a 12-period Exponential Moving Average or EMA to obtain the classic version of the MACD indicator initially recommended by Appel. Nevertheless, the lengths of the moving averages can be varied to better fit a particular currency pair.

In addition, a Trigger Line will generally be computed and plotted over the MACD indicator that can generate signals to help a trader identify additional trading opportunities.

Sample Chart of the MACD Indicator

The histogram and signal line of the MACD Indicator are shown in the image below in the indicator box below a bar chart showing the daily exchange rate action for EUR/USD. The chart was obtained from the MetaTrader5 trading platform.

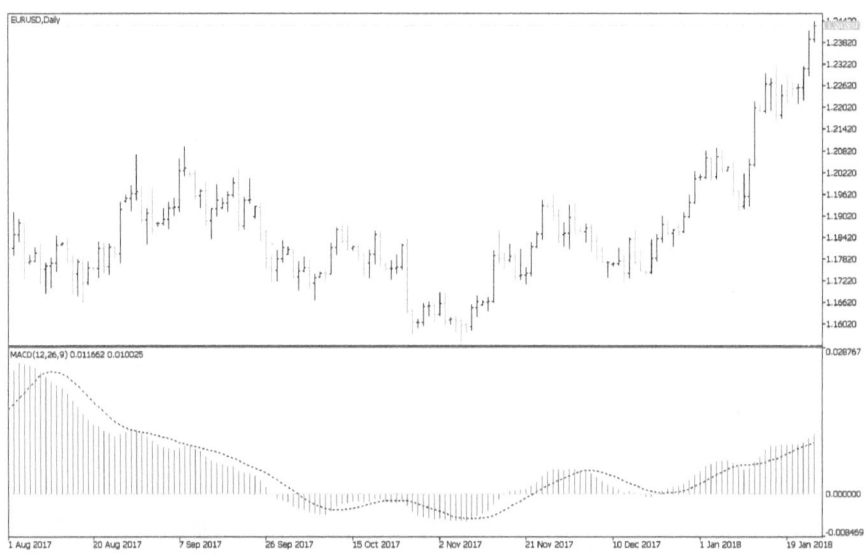

Usage of the MACD Indicator

Traders generally receive the best signals from the MACD indicator when the market trends clearly without trading conditions becoming too choppy. Often, they will look for confirmation from another trading signal before entering a position based on a MACD-based signal.

When observing the MACD indicator in practice, traders typically look for crossovers and the indicator's divergence relative to the price. They can also use the indicator to identify overbought or oversold market conditions ripe for reversals. These signals are explained further below:

- *Crossovers:* One type of crossover on the MACD occurs when the indicator crosses above or below the zero line. When trading such MACD crossovers, the basic rule consists of selling when the indicator falls below zero or buying when it rises above zero. A crossover signal variation involves buying when the MACD moves above its trigger line, or selling when the MACD indicator falls below the trigger line.

- *Divergence:* Divergence happens when extremes in the level of the MACD indicator diverge from those seen in the exchange rate. Divergence often presents a good clue that a market may be nearing a reversal point and it tends to have the greatest importance when occurring at an overbought or oversold price level. Bullish or positive divergence means the MACD makes higher lows when the price is still making lower lows in a down trend. This indicates that the market may be about to reverse to the upside. Conversely, bearish or negative divergence occurs when the MACD makes lower highs when prices continue to make higher highs in an upwards trend. This gives a signal that the market may be ready to reverse and trade downwards.

- *Identifying Overbought and Oversold Market Conditions:* The MACD can also be used to indicate when the market is overbought or oversold. The idea behind this is that when the shorter-term MACD moving average separates or diverges strongly from the longer-term MACD moving average, it indicates an over-extended market. When this situation arises that is characterized by a large absolute value for the MACD indicator, the market probably needs to correct or consolidate before continuing the trend. The market may even reverse direction altogether.

Calculation Method for the MACD Indicator

Technical analysts using the MACD typically calculate its value by subtracting a 26-period exponential moving average's value from that of a 12-period exponential moving average. They will also compute a Trigger line that consists of taking a 9-period simple moving average of the MACD. This line will then be graphed over the MACD.

Definitions:

n	= the number of the time period bar in question.
Close(n)	= The closing price seen during time period n.
SMA(A,B)	= Simple Moving Average of data item A over B periods.
EMA(A,B)	= Exponential Moving Average of data item A over B periods.
SIGNAL	= The MACD's trigger line.

Calculations:

MACD(n) = EMA(Close(n), 12) - EMA(Close(n), 26)

SIGNAL(n) = SMA(MACD(n), 9)

The Market Facilitation Index or MFI Indicator

Bill William's Market Facilitation Index or MFI indicator analyzes the size of the price change or trading range divided by the volume observed for each time period. According to Bill Williams, who wrote about the indicator in his book *Trading Chaos*, the MFI indicator measures "the market's willingness to move the price."

In essence, the Market Facilitation Index provides an estimate of the efficiency of the market in terms of its liquidity and activity. The indicator is also flexible enough to apply to various time frames from 5 minutes upwards.

The MFI indicator is typically graphed using four colors, each of which has significance for traders.

Sample Chart of the MFI Indicator

The histogram of lines in four colors that comprise the MFI Indicator is shown in the image below in the indicator box underneath a bar chart showing the daily exchange rate action for EUR/USD. The chart was obtained from the MetaTrader5 trading platform.

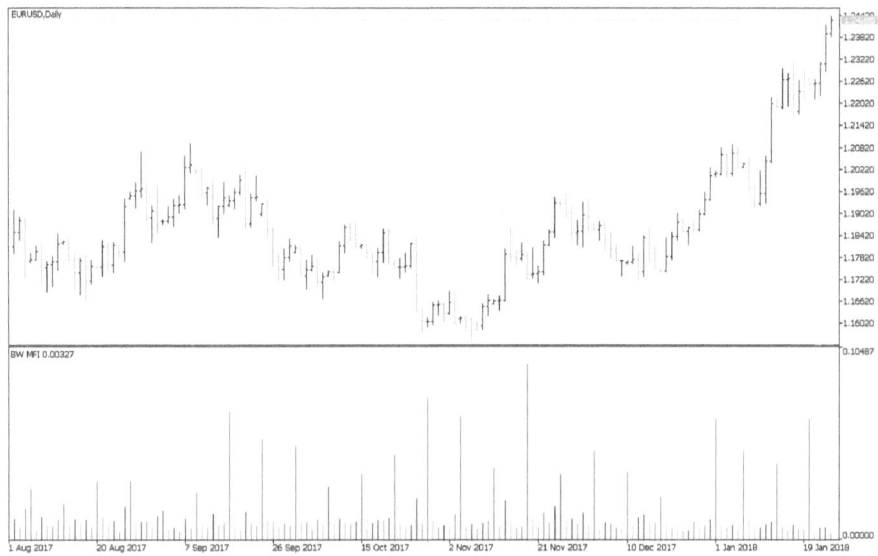

Usage of the MFI Indicator

In practice, Bill Williams identified four states for the Market Facilitation Index that he identified, named and colored as follows:

- **Green Bar or "Green": Both MFI and volume are up**
  Activity rises as more traders enter the market in the direction it is already heading, and the market's movement in that direction is accelerating. This signal confirms the existing trend and indicates you should trade along with it.

- **Blue Bar or "Fake": MFI up but volume down.**
  The market's price continues to further its trend, but volume does not support it. This indicates the move is a fake-out due to speculation and may soon be reversing.

- **Pink (Red) or "Squat": MFI down but volume up.**
  Volume rises as buyers and sellers battle to move the rate, each without much success. This signal indicates a market slowdown after which a breakout may result that could be the start of a new trend. Often, the breakout will occur in the opposite direction from the preceding move.

- **Brown Bar or "Fade": MFI down and volume down.**
  Volume falls as traders get bored with trading the previous trend. This signal indicates the market's interest in the former trend is fading and so traders should look for signs that the market may be building up momentum for a new move.

Calculation Method for the MFI Indicator

The MFI Indicator consists of a histogram in four colors plotted under the price chart. The definitions of the inputs and equations used in its calculation are listed below.

Definitions:

n = the number of the time period bar in question.
High(n) = The high price traded during time period n.
Low(n) = The low price traded during time period n.
MFI(n) = Market Facilitation Index for time period n.
Volume(n) = Trading volume for time period n.

Calculations:

$MFI(n) = [High(n) - Low(n)] / Volume(n)$

The Moving Average or MA Indicator

A Moving Average or MA is a technical indicator that shows the average value of a financial instrument or commodity over a set period of time. The MAs will generally be plotted directly over the price action they are calculated for, and can also be computed on other indicators.

Many technical traders use a relatively simple analytic technique involving moving averages to generate trading signals and follow trends. Moving averages consist of an average of observed exchange rates or prices taken over a set time period that then itself progresses or moves through time.

While traders often simply compute moving averages based on closing prices, other more complicated methods exist that can take the daily ranges into account. The end result of this calculation plotted over time forms a smooth line that tends to lag behind the actual levels observed in the market.

The four major types of moving averages that are in common usage among traders are:

- *Simple Moving Average or SMA* – this type of moving average is calculated by adding the closing price of the instrument for a set number of periods and then dividing the total by the number of periods.

- *Exponential Moving Average or EMA* – an exponential moving average is the same as a simple moving average except that the more recent data is given more weight while older data is decreased exponentially.

- *Smoothed Moving Average or SMMA* – combines elements of both the simple moving average and the exponential moving average. The SMMA gives equal weighting to recent prices as to historic prices. Nevertheless, the calculation does not have a fixed period reference but instead takes all available data into account. Subtracting the previous day's smoothed moving average from the present price and adding the result to the previous day's smoothed moving average will give you the present smoothed moving average.

- *Linear Weighted Moving Average or LWMA* - this MA is calculated by taking all of the price entries over the time period and then multiplying each one by the position of that particular data point and then dividing the number by the sum of the number of periods. In other words, in a 3-day weighted average, today's price would be multiplied by 3, yesterday's price by 2 and then they would be added to the day before yesterday's price, and then that sum would be divided by the sum of the multipliers.

Moving averages are generally lagging indicators and are most effective in identifying and confirming trends as well as identifying major support and resistance levels. In order to help discern whether an instrument is trending or ranging, using the MAs in combination with a trend indicator such as the ADX or Average Directional Index may improve results.

Sample Chart for the Moving Average Indicator

A Simple Moving Average Indicator is shown in the image below superimposed over a bar chart showing the daily exchange rate action for EUR/USD. The chart was obtained from the MetaTrader5 trading platform.

Usage of the Moving Average Indicator

Many traders find Moving Averages extremely useful technical indicators, and they are employed for a variety of different purposes in technical analysis. The main reason traders use moving averages is to identify and confirm trends. Direction, location and crossover are the three principal methods involving Moving Averages that are used to identify trends.

The first technique for identifying a trend using MAs is direction. If the MA is rising, then the market would be considered to be in an up-trend over the time period covered by the Moving Average. Conversely, if the MA is declining, then the trend would be considered down for that period.

The second technique for using MAs to determine trend is price location. If the price of the financial instrument is above the moving average, then the trend would be considered upwards-moving. Conversely, if the price of the instrument is below the moving average, then the trend would be considered downwards-moving.

The third technique involves computing a set of two moving averages, one of shorter duration than the other, or just using the price in combination with a single moving average. If the shorter-term MA or price is above the longer-term MA, then the trend is considered up. If the shorter-term MA or price is below the longer-term MA, then the trend would be considered down.

Technical traders using one or more moving averages to generate trading signals for their trade plans to follow will often observe crossings between the levels of either:

(1) The price and a chosen moving average or

(2) Between a pair of shorter-term and longer-term moving averages.

The signal for such a trader to take a long position comes when the level of the price or shorter-term moving average crosses upward above the other moving average used in the analysis. Conversely, a short signal gets generated when a downward cross-over arises.

When organizing price charts using more than one moving average, it generally makes sense to place them in different colors so that you can easily distinguish the shorter-term moving average from the longer-term average at a glance.

Calculation Method for the Moving Average Indicators

The Moving Average Indicator consists of a line superimposed over the price chart. When learning how to computing moving averages, most traders will start with the calculation for the simple moving average. The equations for the exponential and weighted moving averages are considerably more complex.

Nevertheless, the EMAs and Weighted MAs generally give more weight to more recent price data to reduce the lag of the indicator relative to current market levels and thereby increase the relevance of the average and the timeliness of its trading signals.

The definitions of the inputs and equations used in its calculation for the most common averaging methods are listed below.

Definitions:

n = the number of the time period bar in question.
N = the number of time periods in the averaging process.
Close(n) = The closing price at the end of time period n.

SMA(n)   = Simple Moving Average of price over n periods.
EMA(n)   = Exponential Moving Average of price over n periods.
LWMA(n)   = Weighted Moving Average of price over n periods.
P   = The percent of the exponential moving average.
SUM(n, N) = the sum of N weighting coefficients at time period n.

Calculations:

Simple Moving Average or SMA

A simple moving average is also known as an arithmetical average and involves adding the closing prices over a certain number of individual time periods, and then dividing by the number of periods.

SMA(n) = SUM(Close(n), N) / N

Exponential Moving Average or EMA

A P-percent exponential moving average at time period n is calculated as follows:

EMA(n) = (Close(n) * P) + (EMA(n - 1) * (100 - P))

Smoothed Moving Average SMMA

SMMA(n) = [SMMA(n - 1) * (N - 1) + Close(n)] / N

Linear Weighted Moving Average or LWMA

LWMA(n) = SUM(Close(n)*n, N) / SUM(n, N)

The On Balance Volume or OBV Indicator

The On Balance Volume or OBV indicator was originally introduced in 1963 by Joe Granville in his book *Granville's New Key to Stock Market Profits*. OBV was one of the first indicators to measure positive and negative volume flows in the stock market.

The indicator uses the relatively simple concept that volume precedes price. The indicator is calculated by adding the volume traded if the market closes up and subtracting the volume traded if the market closes down.

By totaling the additions and subtractions of volume, a single OBV line is formed which can then be compared to a price chart of the security to identify confirmations and divergences.

Sample Chart for the OBV Indicator

An OBV Indicator is shown in the image below in the indicator box underneath a bar chart showing the daily exchange rate action for EUR/USD. The chart was obtained from the MetaTrader5 trading platform.

Usage of the OBV Indicator

The basic premise of the On Balance Volume Indicator is that changes in the OBV will precede price changes. Rising volume in a depressed instrument will signal that the instrument has begun a phase of accumulation and the smart money is getting long.

Once additional interest comes into the market and begins buying, the price will most likely rise. Conversely, if the market has been rising for a period of time and an increase in volume ensues at the top of the price range, this means the smart money is selling and the price level has achieved a point of exhaustion. Public selling is usually not far behind.

The OBV indicator also offers directional information. A rising OBV indicates a bullish trend with heavier volume on up days, while a declining OBV indicates a downtrend with heavier volume on down days.

Nevertheless, if prices are rising while volume is declining, then a negative divergence is forming and the up-trend is in serious trouble and cannot be sustained. The same holds true if prices fall on contracting volume. The decline slowly exhausts the selling pressure and a divergence for an up-move starts forming.

Numerical values do not have great significant for this indicator. Instead, the direction of the trend is what to look out for with the OBV indicator, in addition to the relationship between the market price and the indicator's overall direction.

Calculation Method for the OBV Indicator

The OBV Indicator consists of a single line plotted in an indicator box under the price chart. The definitions of the inputs and equations used in its calculation are listed below.

Definition:
n = the number of the time period bar in question.
Close(n) = The closing price at the end of time period n.
Volume(n) = The volume traded during time period n.
OBV(n) = The On Balance Volume Indicator value at time period n.

Calculation:

If Close(n)>Close(n-1) =>

OBV(n) = OBV(n-1) + Volume(n)

If Close(n)>Close(n-1) =>

OBV(n) = OBV(n-1) - Volume(n)

If Close(n)=Close(n-1) =>

OBV(n) = OBV(n-1)

The Parabolic SAR Indicator

The Parabolic Stop and Reversal or Parabolic SAR technical indicator was developed by J. Welles Wilder who also created the RSI and ADX indicators. Usually displayed as a chart overlay indicator, Parabolic SAR helps traders set trailing stops during trending markets.

The Parabolic SAR indicator is related to Moving Averages, but it moves with a higher acceleration rate and can "turn" or switch position above and below the price. When the Parabolic SAR is below the market that indicates an upwards trend, and when it is below the market that indicates a downward trend prevails.

Whenever the market price moves over the Parabolic SAR dots, the indicator turns and starts accumulating values on the other side of the price. The starting point for such turns becomes the high or low price for the preceding period. Also, due to its acceleration factor, the faster the price rises or falls, the faster the Parabolic SAR indicator moves toward the price action.

Sample Chart of the Parabolic SAR Indicator

A Parabolic SAR Indicator is shown in the image below as a series of dots superimposed over a bar chart showing the daily exchange rate action for EUR/USD. The chart was obtained from the MetaTrader5 trading platform.

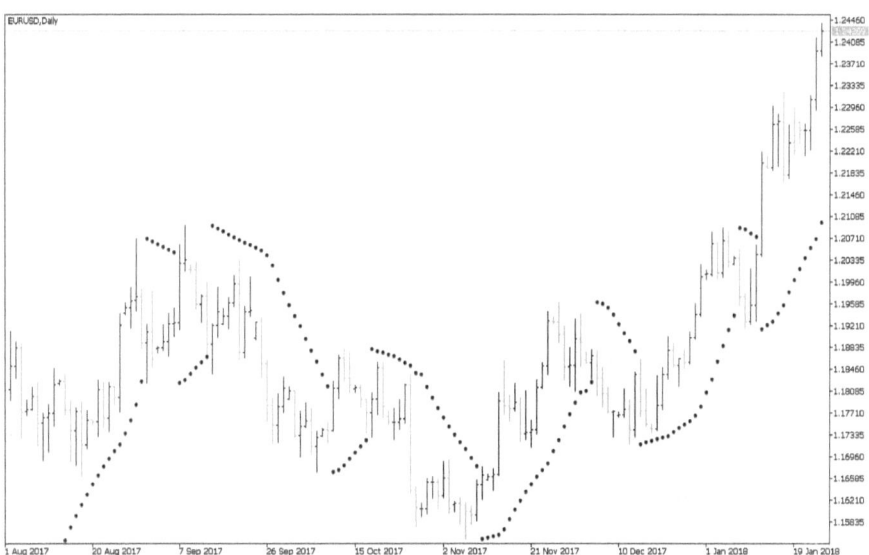

Usage of the Parabolic SAR

The Parabolic SAR Indicator seems to be more popular among traders for setting stops than for indicating what trend direction prevails. In fact, Wilder recommended establishing the trend direction first, and then using Parabolic SAR to help follow it.

When the trend moves upward, you can use the indicator to signal a buy as soon as it turns under the price. Conversely, when the trend moves downward, it will signal a sell trade as it moves up over the price. The turn of the Parabolic SAR indicator signals the end of the prevailing trend and its possible reversal.

Many traders use the Parabolic SAR to indicate suitable exit points for trend-following systems. Often, they will close a long position when the price moves below the SAR line, while shorts get closed if the price rallies over the SAR line. In this case, the indicator basically serves as a useful signal of where to execute trailing stops.

Calculation Method for the Parabolic SAR

The Parabolic SAR Indicator consists of a series of dots plotted either above or below the price action on a price chart to signal either a short or long position respectively. The definitions of the inputs and equations used in its calculation are listed below.

Definition:

n = the number of the time period bar in question.
$High(n)$ = The high price traded during time period n.
$Low(n)$ = The low price traded during time period n.
$SAR(n-1)$ = the value of the SAR for the previous bar before bar n.
$Acceleration$ = the acceleration factor.
$Eprice(n-1)$ = the highest or lowest price for the previous period
$Eprice(n)$ = $High(n)$ for long positions or $Low(n)$ for short positions.

Calculations:

$SAR(n) = SAR(n-1) + Acceleration \cdot [Eprice(n-1) - SAR(n-1)]$

The Relative Strength Index or RSI Indicator

The Relative Strength Index or RSI was first introduced in 1978 by J. Welles Wilder in his book *New Concepts in Technical Trading Systems*. Since that time, the Relative Strength Index has become one of the most popular and widely-used momentum oscillators and forms a key part of many trading systems.

The Relative Strength Index oscillator gives a reading between 0 and 100 and is calculated by comparing the magnitude of a market's recent price advances to the magnitude of its recent declines. The indicator requires one parameter which is the number of time periods used in the calculation. The most common value for this is 14 time periods, as was recommended by Wilder.

Sample Chart of the RSI Indicator

An RSI Indicator is shown in the image below in the indicator box underneath a bar chart showing the daily exchange rate action for EUR/USD. The chart was obtained from the MetaTrader5 trading platform.

Usage of the RSI Indicator

Perhaps the most common usage of the Relative Strength Index oscillator involves its ability to indicate overbought and oversold levels, with 70 being the minimum overbought level and 30 being the maximum oversold level. If the RSI goes above 30, then it would be a bullish signal and if it dropped below 70, it would indicate a bearish signal.

RSI divergences relative to the market price are also used as a trading signal generator. When the RSI shows a divergence with the underlying instrument, the divergence will often precede a change in the price's direction.

Another creative way of using the RSI involves looking for chart patterns, trend line breaks or support and resistance points on the RSI graph, just as you would on a price chart.

Finally, a crossover of the RSI's centerline, which has a standard value of 50, can have a bullish or bearish connotation. In general, readings above 50 indicate that average gains are higher than average losses, while readings below 50 indicate that average gains are smaller than average losses.

Calculation Method for the RSI Indicator

The RSI Indicator consists of a single line plotted in an indicator box under the price chart that ranges between 0 and 100. The definitions of the inputs and equations used in its calculation are listed below.

Definitions:

n	= the number of the time period bar in question.
N	= the number of time periods in the averaging process.
$U(n,N)$	= the average number of positive price changes over N time periods at time n.
$D(n,N)$	= the average number of negative price changes over N time periods at time n.
$RSI(n)$	= The Relative Strength Index value at time period n.

Calculations:

$$RSI(n) = 100 - [\, 100 / (1 + U(n,N) / D(n,N)\,)\,]$$

The Relative Vigor Index or RVI Indicator

The Relative Vigor Index or RVI technical indicator is based on the assumption that in a bull market the closing price will usually be higher than the opening price, and conversely in a bear market the closing price will be below the opening price.

The RVI oscillator measures the vigor, or energy, of the move as determined by where the markets finishes. The indicator can also be smoothed by a simple moving average, with 10 being a popular number of periods.

A signal line can also be computed for the RVI as a moving average of four periods on the oscillator values. This reduces price fluctuations and smoothes the curve even further.

Sample Chart of the RVI Indicator

An RVI Indicator is shown in the image below in the indicator box underneath a bar chart showing the daily exchange rate action for EUR/USD. The chart was obtained from the MetaTrader5 trading platform.

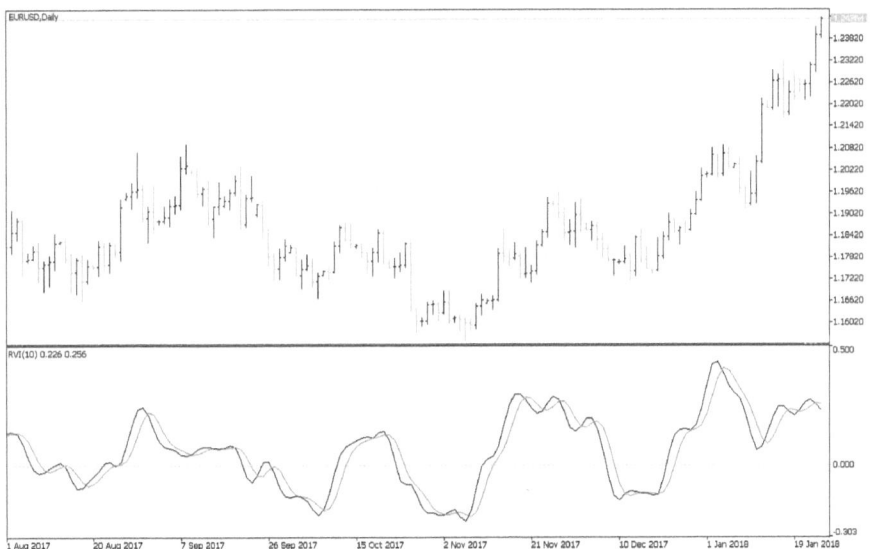

Usage of the RVI Indicator

Perhaps the most important signal generated by the Relative Vigor Index involves a clue that the current trend is weakening based on the occurrence of divergence of the indicator with the market price action.

Bullish divergence means the RVI indicator does not make a new low even though the price does. Bearish divergence, on the other hand, occurs when the RVI does not hit a new high despite the price making one. Each of these events signals weakness in the energy of the current trend.

Furthermore, a crossover of the signal line by the RVI line once the bullish or bearish divergence becomes apparent on the chart can be used as an indicator to initiate either a long or short position. The direction depends on whether the divergence is bullish, in which case a long is taken, or bearish, which would suggest a short position.

Finally, if the overbought or oversold condition for the RVI indicator is breached in a flat market, this also provides a buy or sell signal, depending on which side the break occurs on.

Calculation Method of the RVI Indicator

The RVI Indicator consists of two lines plotted in an indicator box under the price chart that have no set range. The definitions of the inputs and equations used in its calculation are listed below.

Define:
- n = the number of the time period bar in question.
- High(n) = The high price traded during time period n.
- Low(n) = The low price traded during time period n.
- Open(n) = The opening price at the start of time period n.
- Close(n) = The closing price at the end of time period n.
- RVI(n) = The Relative Vigor Index value at time period n.

Calculate:

RVI(n) = (Close(n) − Open(n)) / (High(n) − Low(n))

The Stochastic Oscillator Indicator

The Stochastic Oscillator Indicator, sometimes just referred to as the Stochastics Indicator, has considerable similarities to the Williams %R oscillator. The Stochastic Oscillator was originally developed by George C. Lane in the late 1950s to assist traders in identifying when the market is trading near overbought or oversold extreme points.

In essence, the Stochastic Oscillator indicator plots the relationship of the market's close relative to the high-low range seen over a chosen number of time periods. When the market regularly closes near the top of the indicator's range, this indicates buying pressure or accumulation. Similarly, when a string of closes that approach the indicator's range bottom appear, that indicates selling pressure or distribution is occurring.

Three types of Stochastic Oscillators can be found in common usage. These are the Fast, Slow and Full Stochastics which each have %K and %D lines. %K relates to the market's close relative to the high-low range seen over a chosen number of time periods, while %D is a moving average of %K used to generate trading signals.

The Slow Stochastic just takes a moving average of the Fast Stochastic to help smooth out false signals, while the third type, the Full Stochastic just takes in a third parameter to avoid doing this extra step. The indicator's scale customarily ranges from 0 to 100, and it gives an oversold reading for levels from 20 to 0 and an overbought reading for levels seen between 80 and 100.

Sample Chart of the Stochastics Indicator

A Stochastics Indicator is shown in the image below in the indicator box underneath a bar chart showing the daily exchange rate action for EUR/USD. The chart was obtained from the MetaTrader5 trading platform.

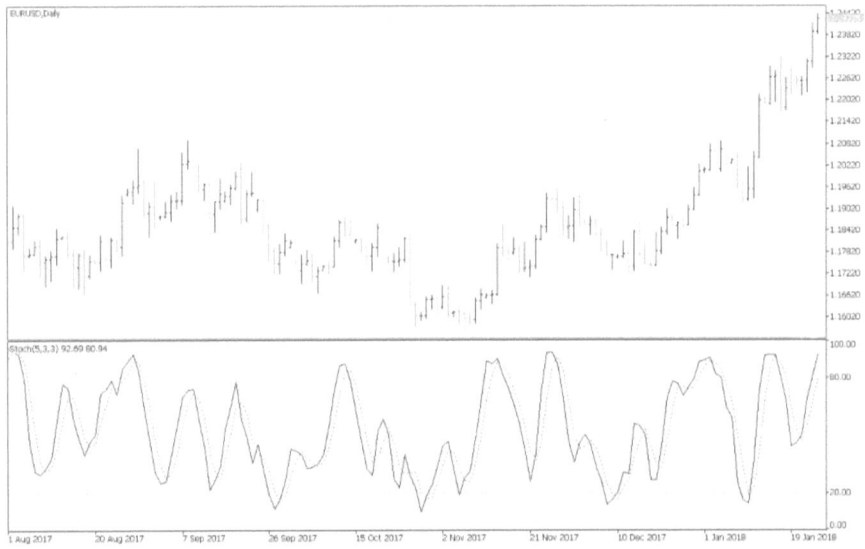

Usage of the Stochastics Indicator

When using the Stochastic Oscillator, most traders consider readings seen over 80 to be overbought and those under 20 to be oversold.

Nevertheless, that does not yet indicate a coming reversal. Instead, one should ideally look for the market to cross back into neutral territory before generating a trade signal.

In addition, the Stochastics Oscillator can be used to generate trading signals whenever the %K line moves above the %D line for a buy, or below the %D line for a sell. Nevertheless, this method can make several unsuccessful trades before it indicates one that succeeds. This disadvantage can be overcome by looking for a divergence between the price and the oscillator in overbought or oversold territory.

For a sell signal based on divergence, this means that the price has still made two higher highs with the Stochastics above 80 for both, but the second high on the Stochastics was not as high as the first. For the corresponding buy signal, the price would be making lower lows, and the Stochastics are below 20 for each, but the second did not make a new low on the Stochastics.

Calculation Method for the Stochastics Indicator

The Stochastics Indicator consists of two lines plotted in an indicator box under the price chart that range between 0 and 100. The definitions of the inputs and equations used in its calculation are listed below.

Definitions:

n = the number of the time period bar in question.
N = the number of time periods for observing highs and lows.
N1 = the number of time periods used in the smoothing process for fast Stochastics.
N2 = the number of time periods used in the smoothing process for slow Stochastics.
N3 = the number of time periods used in the smoothing process for full Stochastics.
High(N,n) = The highest high price seen over N time periods at time n.
Low(N,n) = The lowest low price seen over N time periods at time n.
Close(n) = The closing price at the end of time period n.
SMA(A,B) = Simple Moving Average of data item A over B periods.
%K(n) = The first Fast Stochastics line.
%D(n) = The second Fast Stochastics line.
%KSLOW(n) = The first Slow Stochastics line.

%DSLOW(n) = The second Slow Stochastics line.
%KFULL(n) = The first Full Stochastics line.
%DFULL(n) = The second Full Stochastics line.

Calculations:

For Fast Stochastics:

$\%K(n) = [Close(n) - Low(N,n)]/[High(N,n)-Low(N,n)]*100$

$\%D(n) = SMA(\%K(n), N1)$

For Slow Stochastics:

$\%KSLOW(n) = SMA(\%K(n), 3)$

$\%DSLOW(n) = SMA(\%KSLOW, N2)$

For Full Stochastics

$\%KFULL(n) = SMA(\%K(n), N2)$

$\%DFULL(n) = SMA(\%KFULL(n), N3)$

The Williams' Percent Range or %R Indicator

The Williams' Percent Range technical indicator, sometimes referred to as the Williams %R or just the %R oscillator, has considerable similarities to the Stochastic Oscillator. This useful oscillator was originally developed by Larry Williams to help traders identify when the market is nearing overbought or oversold extremes.

In essence, the Williams %R indicator plots the relationship of the market's closing price relative to the range seen over a given time frame. The indicator's scale customarily ranges from 0 to -100, and it gives an overbought reading for levels from -20 to 0 and an oversold reading for levels between -80 to -100.

The %R indicator also has an especially good reputation for turning down just before a major peak or turning up just before a major low, making it a useful leading technical indicator of price action.

Sample Chart of the Williams' %R Indicator

A Williams' %R Indicator is shown in the image below in the indicator box underneath a bar chart showing the daily exchange rate action for EUR/USD. The chart was obtained from the MetaTrader5 trading platform.

Usage of the Williams' %R Indicator

The most common usage for the Williams %R indicator among traders is to identify extreme price action where the market is overbought or oversold as follows:

Overbought: Between 0 and -20
Neutral: Between -20 and -80
Oversold: Between -80 and -100

Most traders using the Williams Percent Range indicator also prefer to wait until the market price action has reversed direction prior to establishing a position based on this indicator.

For example, if the Williams %R shows a reading of -15, you would not sell into that strength until the price had shown some downside action first. One way to do this would be to wait for it to return from overbought territory and sell at the point where it crosses the -20 boundary.

Calculation Method for the Williams' %R Indicator

The Williams' %R Indicator consists of a single line plotted in an indicator box under the price chart that range between 0 and -100. The definitions of the inputs and equations used in its calculation are listed below.

Definitions:

n	= the number of the time period bar in question.
N	= the number of time periods observed.
High(N,n)	= The highest high price seen over N time periods at time n.
Low(N,n)	= The lowest low price seen over N time periods at time n.
Close(n)	= The closing price at the end of time period n.
%R(n)	= The Williams Percent Range at time period n.

Calculations:

%R(n) = [High(N,n)-Close(n)]/[High(N,n)-Low(N,n)]*100

CHAPTER 6: RECOMMENDED FURTHER READING

As endeavors, trading, and the market analysis that drives it, both go back to the age-old beginning of commerce. Fortunately, many successful traders throughout the years have written about their experiences — including both their brilliant successes and glaring mistakes — so that those newer to trading thankfully do not need to repeat them.

To start with, if you plan on trading via an exchange or online broker, then they should provide websites that their clients can view with details about each asset and contract you are interested in trading. You should review those contract specifications carefully to make sure you understand the quantities involved and the maturity date before executing a single trade.

Another important practical matter involves understanding the delivery requirements if a contract cannot be cash settled, and this can be especially important for commodity traders.

Further Readings on Technical Analysis

After reading this book on technical analysis, most seasoned traders would agree that an excellent reference book on technical analysis is "Technical Analysis of the Financial Markets: A Comprehensive Guide to Trading Methods and Applications" by John G. Murphy.

This classic book gives a detailed overview of all major chart patterns and technical indicators, and it remains an invaluable resource for both new and professional traders interested in technical analysis.

In addition, reading books that go into depth on particular aspects of technical analysis that you are most interested in will give newer traders deeper insights into this important market analysis discipline that lie beyond the scope of this introductory book to the topic.

Readings on Fundamental Analysis

Although many other books are available on the subject of trading and market analysis, be sure that your reading on the subject also includes a well-rounded treatment of fundamental analysis, since technical analysis alone is rarely sufficient if you really want to understand why financial markets move.

For further education on the topic of fundamental analysis as it relates to trading, the reader is first referred to the other book in this financial markets analysis series on that subject by the same authors, entitled "Fundamental Analysis for Financial Markets Traders". In addition to discussing fundamental analysis in general and how to perform it, the book covers fundamental topics specific to the forex, stock and commodity markets and contains an extensive reference section on fundamental economic indicators.

Books on Trading in General

If you happen to be new to trading, these same professional authors and traders have penned three comprehensive introductory guides to trading each of the top three financial markets that provide you with all the information you need to start trading. Respectively entitled: "Forex Trading: A Beginner's Guide", "Stock Trading: A Beginner's Guide" and "Commodity Trading: A Beginner's Guide", these books were recently published in three self-sufficient volumes within the authors' Beginner's Guides to Financial Markets Trading series. Each book is currently available for purchase at Amazon.com in paperback and Kindle formats at very reasonable prices.

Beyond that, a broader list of recommended literature should probably include books on trading in general, because regardless of what financial market you are watching, trading or analyzing, traders of every discipline share the same overall experience.

The first book on trading that comes to mind would have to be "Reminiscences of a Stock Operator" by Edwin Lefevre. Based on the life of Jesse Livermore, this classic book captures the attitudes and mindset of one of the most successful stock traders of the first half of the 20th century. Although the stock market was still young then, the book still gives you a good idea of what goes on in the mind of a remarkably successful trader. Although Livermore traded stocks, many of his experiences and his mindset are very relevant to commodity traders.

Two more recent bestsellers provide a useful perspective on trading for aspiring or seasoned traders alike. "The Market Wizards" and "The New Market Wizards" by Jack Schwager both contain excellent interviews with some of the world's top traders. Together, they give extraordinary insight both into the traders' psychology, as well as into how to profit in specific markets and how such top market players developed their trading systems.

Another fascinating book on trading is "The Complete Turtle Trader" by Michael Covel. The book recounts the famous story of the Turtles — a group of traders that were trained in trend-following by master trader Richard Dennis. He began this experiment as a result of a bet made with colleague William Eckhardt, and it became wildly successful. Nevertheless, some of the subjects of the experiment were not as profitable as others given the same opportunity. The book also lays out the principles and trading rules of the experiment and offers highly-educational reading for anyone serious about trading.

Further Reading on Market Analysis and Trading

In addition to the aforementioned books by these authors published by Jellyhawk Financial Press, many other fine books on market analysis and trading can be found, and the New York Institute of Finance publishes an especially good collection of books on those topics.

Remember, the more you know about the subject of trading and how to analyze the financial markets you have chosen to participate in, the more prepared you will be when you make decisions as a trader.

Basically, when it comes to trading, knowledge really is power, and knowing how to apply that knowledge consistently and in a disciplined manner generally distinguishes successful traders and market analysts from the rest of the pack.

ABOUT THE AUTHORS

Jay and Julie Hawk are a husband and wife team who currently trade forex, stocks, commodities and cryptocurrencies online for their own account and have worked professionally in the financial markets in several different occupations. Together, they have more than 40 years of experience trading in the financial markets and are world-class experts at performing both technical and fundamental analysis to support their trading and risk management activities.

For her part, Julie completed her scientific research degree and started out working as a business systems analyst for a major investment bank where she became qualified as a Series 7 Registered Representative and was thoroughly trained in all major financial products. She also attended the well-known O'Connell and Piper options training course in Chicago. She soon started working as a dealer in the trading rooms of several major international banks in New York City, London and San Francisco, eventually working her way up to the vice president level.

In that capacity, Julie was personally involved in educating, providing customized hedging and risk taking strategies, meeting with other corporate executives, and handling large scale transactions for high-profile banking clients including large corporations, fund managers and high net worth individuals. She also traded substantial options portfolios for her employers as a risk manager, including exotic options like binary, barrier, average rate and basket options. She even received a notable award for her creativity, teamwork and profitability in executing unusual and highly profitable derivatives transactions.

During that time, Julie also developed high level expertise in technical analysis, including Elliott Wave Theory, and was involved in initiating research into automated trading and trading signal systems. She also joined the San Francisco Writers' Guild and regularly wrote trade strategies, educational material, market commentary, market newsletters, reports, articles and press releases. In addition, Julie was interviewed for various financial markets magazines and for news wires such as REUTERS in her professional capacity as a financial markets expert.

In contrast to Julie's highly professional and elite banking role, Jay's professional trading experience was focused more on futures and options exchange floor trading activities, fund management, and fundamental research-based commodity trading and stock investing. After growing up in Chicago and then moving to Mexico City, Jay returned to Chicago to begin working in the futures and options markets on the Chicago Board Options Exchange just a few years after the exchange was founded.

In addition to working his way up to holding a seat and operating as a market maker on several options exchanges in Chicago and San Francisco, Jay also ran a retail stock brokerage desk and managed funds for a number of large institutional investors that he traded profitably on a discretionary basis and that included stock, commodity and forex trades. Jay later took a position on the Chicago Mercantile Exchange where he helped start up and actively traded in a variety of listed futures and options. He eventually moved to the West Coast to start trading on the Pacific Options Exchange, where he focused largely on trading stock options and the underlying stocks.

After both independently retiring from their professional trading careers as relatively wealthy people, Jay and Julie met up, fell love and got married to raise a child together just after the new millennium dawned. They moved to Mexico to semi-retire near the beach and operate an Internet-based business together, but they soon discovered that the financial markets had become far more accessible to retail traders via online brokers and the availability of CFD trading. This incredible opportunity seemed too tempting for these seasoned traders to ignore!

They also observed a demand for educational material to be provided to retail traders via the Internet, and that the quality of existing written content available online was rather poor. That led them to start a new career together as freelance writers specializing in writing about the financial markets using their professional background and expertise. This eventually resulted in them co-founding TheFXperts (located online at www.thefxperts.com) to provide clients with expertly-written market analysis and commentary, informational content about financial markets, trader mentoring and account management. They also presently act as advisors to Support and Resist (located online at www.supportandresist.com), which provides fully automated trading solutions, custom indicators and trading signal software to retail and professional trading clients.

Jay and Julie are very pleased to present this book on technical analysis as the second in a two-part series of books on financial markets analysis to supplement their existing three volume guide to trading the forex, stock and commodity markets. You can visit TheFXperts' website at www.thefxperts.com to learn about their current books and future releases.

GLOSSARY

Bar Chart: A graphic representation of the price of an asset or financial instrument with entries in the form of a bar. Each bar represents the open, high, low and close of the price during a specified period of time. The bars on the chart form patterns that give the technical analyst indications of the future price of the asset or financial instrument.

Candlestick Chart: A graphic representation of the price of an asset or financial instrument originally from Japan that uses "candlesticks" as entries. The candlestick is formed within a specified time period with the opening price indicating if the candle is an "up" candle or a "down" candle, typically using black to represent a downward movement and white for an upward movement. The opening and closing price, which generally form a long box represent what is known as the "body" of the candle. "Shadows" or "wicks" are the lines that extend from the top or bottom of the body representing the range that the asset traded in outside of the opening and closing prices.

Chart Pattern: An identifiable form composed of bars or other entries that represent the trading price of an asset or commodity on a graph. In technical analysis, chart patterns are used as indications of the likely future movements of the price of financial assets.

Channel: Two upward or downward sloping parallel lines that contain the graphical representation of the price action of an asset or financial instrument on a price chart.

Closing Price: The final closing amount of money at which an asset has traded at on a given trading day. In markets that trade round the clock, the closing price is determined at a certain hour of the day for the region in which the asset is traded. For example, the CME closes commodity futures trading each weekday at 5:00pm EST and then re-opens for electronic trading at 6pm EST.

Cross Rate: The exchange rate between two currencies neither of which is the U.S. Dollar. EUR/JPY and GBP/EUR are two common cross rates.

Currency Futures: Standardized foreign exchange contracts traded on centralized exchanges that involve the purchase of one currency and the sale of another. The delivery date for such transferrable contracts usually falls on particular date, often quarterly, in order to provide greater liquidity, and the futures trade in amounts that are multiples of the standard lot size for the contract.

Currency: The primary unit of payment and hence the means by which trade occurs in a particular country. Physical currency can be made of either paper or coin, and it is usually issued by the country's government to serve as money within its borders.

Dealing Spread: The difference or spread between the immediate prices at which a dealer, broker or market maker is willing to buy and sell a particular commodity or other asset. The dealing spread is composed of a low bid price and a higher offer price which respectively represent where a market maker is willing to buy and sell the asset.

Exchange Rate: The exchange rate or rate of exchange is the market-determined amount of the base or primary currency expressed in units of the counter or secondary currency. Typically, an exchange rate would be quoted for delivery in two business days or value spot.

Foreign Exchange Market: The forum in which participants buy and sell currencies against each other. Participants include central banks, commercial and investment banks, corporations, fund managers, hedge funds and personal forex traders.

Foreign Exchange Option: A contract that confers upon its buyer the right, but not the obligation, to enter into a foreign exchange contract at a particular price and date in the future for a price known as the premium. They are usually specified by their currency pair, strike price, expiration date, direction and amount. Most currency options traded are customized contracts dealt in the over-the-counter forex market, although standardized forex options trade on the Chicago IMM and Philadelphia Stock Exchanges.

Foreign Exchange: A transaction whereby the currency of one country is exchanged or traded for the currency of another country. Typically, this foreign exchange trade is done at a particular rate and for value "spot" or delivery of the two currencies in two business days, except for USD/CAD which typically delivers in just one business day.

Forex: A shortened form of the phrase "foreign exchange" that refers to transactions whereby the currency of one country is exchanged or traded for the currency of another country. Typically, this trade will be done at a particular rate of exchange and for value "spot" which is delivery of the two currencies in two business days, except for USD/CAD which typically delivers in just one business day.

Fundamental Analysis: A method of research that involves determining a commodity or other asset's intrinsic value by investigating the related financial and economic factors that influence its valuation. These factors could be related to the supply, demand, production and company's management, macro or microeconomic data and would determine if the security or asset is fairly valued, undervalued or overvalued.

Futures Contract: A standardized and transferable agreement traded on an exchange the price of which depends on that of an underlying asset. The delivery dates for such futures contracts will generally fall on a particular set of dates, often quarterly, in order to provide greater liquidity. Futures trade in amounts that are multiples of the standard lot size for the contract.

Futures Market: Refers to a system for trading futures contracts, which are agreements to transact a certain amount of a commodity on a future date. Futures markets consist of centralized exchanges located in various countries that are part of the overall commodities market.

High: The highest level that the price of an asset or financial instrument has traded at in a specified time period. Technical analysts generally use the high of the day, week or month when working out levels of support and resistance.

Indicator: In technical analysis, an indicator is a type of metric determined by the price action of an asset or financial instrument that is used to predict the general direction of future prices. Indicators most used in technical analysis consist of oscillators, relative strength indexes and moving averages, to name just a few.

Indicator Box: A section of a financial chart containing the graphic representation of an indicator's behavior. An indicator box could be located right under a price chart with volume figures or the relative strength index for example.

Leverage: In finance, leverage is the use of debt for the financing of an activity. For example, an individual paying for a property with a mortgage or a company that has more than 80 percent debt relative to its assets would be considered leveraged. In commodities trading, leverage is achieved by using margin, which calls for a fraction of funds to be deposited in a margin account in order to control the purchase or short sale of securities.

Line Chart: A graphical representation of the price of an asset or financial instrument using the last price in a specified period to form a line on the graph. Line charts have a limited amount of information and are not often used by technical analysts.

Low: The lowest level that the price of an asset or financial instrument has traded at in a specified time period. Technical analysts generally use the low of the day, week or month when working out levels of support and resistance.

Margin: A collateral amount used in the purchase or sale of futures contracts or CFDs. The margin for a purchase consists of the collateral amount that the buyer of the instrument needs to put up with the broker to cover the amount of risk of the transaction. For example, for the purchase of Heating Oil futures contracts worth $100,000, a margin deposit of 20 percent of the total notional amount or $20,000 is required by the broker or exchange to make the purchase.

Market Close: The end of a trading session for any particular market. For example, the market close of the Chicago Mercantile Exchange occurs each weekday at 5:00PM Eastern Standard Time. A closed market refers to exchange holidays when no trading takes place.

Market Index: A market metric that consists of the weighted values of components included in a particular list of companies. A stock market index shows the performance of a group of component stocks weighted according to their shares outstanding and share price in a mathematical formula, for example the Dow Jones Industrial Average, an index which shows the performance of the 30 top U.S. industrial stocks.

Market Maker: An individual who makes two way prices on certain commodities, usually to clients or on exchanges. They may also watch and execute orders for clients.

Open Interest: In the futures and options market, the amount of contracts of a monthly cycle (futures) or a specified series (options) that are outstanding. In the futures market, open interest can indicate levels of supply and demand, while in the options market, a large open interest in a particular strike will attract the price to that level as the options expiration date approaches.

Oscillator: A tool used by technical analysts that employs two extreme values that, along with a trend indicator can determine overbought and oversold conditions in the market. When the oscillator rises to the extreme value on the upper end, the asset is considered to be overbought. When the oscillator declines to the lower extreme value, then the asset is considered oversold.

Over-the-Counter or OTC: Refers to a decentralized market in which assets or financial instruments are not traded on an official exchange. In general, such OTC instruments will instead be dealt directly between counterparties over the telephone or via some other reliable means of communicating contractual terms, like an electronic dealing system for example.

Peak: The highest point a price or an indicator has reached on a chart for a particular time period. Peaks and troughs are commonly used by technical analysts to determine possible future price movements.

Price Chart: A graphic representation of the price of an asset or financial instrument during a specified time period. Price charts give technical analysts an indication of where prices are possibly going based on historical data.

Precious Metals: Metallic substances that have a high intrinsic economic value. Such metals are rare and serve as a store of intrinsic wealth for nations and individuals, as well as having various industrial applications. Precious metals include: gold, silver, palladium and platinum. They are traded on many of the world's largest commodity exchanges, such as the New York Mercantile Exchange, the London Metals Exchange and the Chicago Mercantile Exchange.

Range: A set of market prices bounded on the top by the high price and on the bottom by the low price of a futures contract or other asset observed during a particular trading time frame. For example, if WTI Crude Oil had a daily high of $60 per barrel and a daily low of $55 per barrel, then the range of that contract during the trading day was $55-$60.

Retail Foreign Exchange Broker: A financial intermediary that generally caters to individual foreign exchange traders that typically trade currencies in smaller amounts for speculative purposes. Often such brokers offer online trading capabilities and many support automated forex trading.

Retail Forex: A term generally pertaining to individual foreign exchange traders that typically trade currencies in smaller amounts. Such smaller traders will often use technical analysis-based trading methods, and they generally trade forex for speculative purposes.

Resistance: A technical term that refers to an excess of supply of a commodity at a given price level. For example, if a commodity futures contract trades up to $12 per lot after opening at $10, and then trades back to $10, then the resistance level for that particular time frame would be at the $12 price the market reversed at.

Reversal: When the price action of an asset or financial instrument turns around and goes in the opposite direction of the prevailing trend. Reversals tend to happen at major market tops and bottoms; however, small reversals can occur in the market intraday and are monitored by short term traders and scalpers.

Stock Market: Refers to a system for trading stocks, which represent equity or ownership in their issuing corporations. Stocks are traded on centralized and non-centralized stock exchanges that form a part of the overall Stock Market.

Stock Quote: An indication of the market price for the particular stock that the price is being obtained for. A Stock Quote typically comes with a bid price and an offer price, with the difference known as the spread.

Stock: Refers to the shares of a corporation which represent an ownership interest in that corporation. Stocks can be issued privately or can be offered to the public and traded on an exchange.

Support: A technical analysis term that refers to an abundance of buy orders at a certain price level in a commodity or other asset. When its price reaches a level of support, the asset tends to move higher until reaching a level, known as resistance, where an excess of supply puts downward pressure on its price.

Technical Analysis: A method of investigation into the price patterns of commodities or other assets that depends on the levels of supply and demand. Technical analysis indicates at what prices assets are most likely to appreciate or decline by using indicators such as oscillators, moving averages and volume figures.

Tick Chart: A graphic representation of a specified number of transaction per entry, typically in the form of a bar. For example, many Forex traders use a 220 tick chart, which means that each bar on the graph represents 220 transactions. As in other bar charts, tick chart bars show the open, high, low and close.

Trend: The prevailing direction of asset prices. For example, an upward trend would indicate that the price of a commodity is gaining, while a downward trend would indicate that its price is falling. Three major trends types can be discerned in an asset market: rising, declining and flat.

Trendline: a graphic representation of the general direction of the price of an asset or financial instrument for a specified period of time. A trendline generally lets the technical analyst know whether the prevailing trend in an asset or financial instrument is up or down in the long, medium or short terms.

Trough: The lowest point a price or an indicator has reached on a chart for a particular time period. Peaks and troughs are commonly used by technical analysts to determine possible future price movements.

Volume: The amount of an asset or financial instrument or the number of shares of stock traded in a specified period of time. Volume is the most reliable measure of supply and demand and an important indicator for technical analysts that often use volume numbers to confirm other indicators.

INDEX

Acceleration/Deceleration, 56
Accumulation/Distribution, 58
Algo Terminal, 52
Alligator, 61
Automated Trading, 50
Automated Trading Software, 49
Average True Range, 66
Awesome Oscillator, 68
Bar Chart, 117
Body, 17
Bollinger Bands, 28, 71
Candlestick Chart, 117
Candlestick Charts, 15
Channel, 117
Channels, 8, 13
Chart Pattern, 7, 9, 117
Charting Service, 33
Closing Price, 118
Commodity Channel Index, 73
Congestion, 15
Consolidation, 9
Continuation, 9
Contracts for Difference, 44
Cross Rate, 118
Currency, 118
Currency Futures, 118
Dealing Spread, 118

Directional Movement Index, 29
Doji, 17
Double Top, 12
Economic Indicators, 1
Edwin Lefevre, 110
Elliot Wave Theory, 23
Envelopes, 76
Exchange Rate, 118
FAP Turbo, 45
Fibonacci Retracement Levels, 15, 25, 26
Fibonacci Sequence, 25
Flats, 23
Force Index, 78
Foreign Exchange, 118, 119, 122
Foreign Exchange Market, 118
Foreign Exchange Option, 118
Forex, 119, 122
Forex Megadroid, 45
Forex Robots, 47
Fractals, 80
Fundamental Analysis, 1, 2, 31, 119
Fundamentals, 3
Further Reading, 109
Futures Contract, 119
Futures Market, 119

Gambling, 1
Head and Shoulders Top, 11
High, 120
Historical Volatility, 28
Homma Munehisa, 16
Human Behavior, 6
Ichimoku Kinko Hyo, 82
Indicator, 120
Indicator Box, 120
Investment Banks, 118
Jack Schwager, 111
Jellyhawk Financial Press, ii, xii, 2, 111
John G. Murphy, 109
Leverage, 120
Line Chart, 120
Low, 120
Lower Shadow, 17
MACD, 28, *See* Moving Average Convergence/Divergence,
Margin, 120
Market Close, 121
Market Facilitation Index, 88
Market Index, 121
Market-makers, 4
Marubozu, 17
MetaTrader, ix, 44, 51
Michael Covel, 111
Momentum Indicator, 29
Moving Average, 90
Moving Average Convergence/Divergence, 28, 85
New York Institute of Finance, 111
News, 4, 5
On Balance Volume, 94
Open Interest, 121
Oscillator, 121
OTC. *See* Over-the-Counter
Over-the-Counter, 121
Parabolic SAR, 96
Pattern-Matching, 48
Peak, 122
Pennants, 10
Pivot Points, 21, 22
Point and Figure Charts, 18
Precious Metals, 122
Price Chart, 122
Price Patterns, 40
Psychological Levels, 15
Range, 122
Range Trading, 35
Real Time Price Quotes, 45
Rectangles, 11
Relative Strength Index, 27, 98
Relative Vigor Index, 100
Resistance, 122
Resistance Levels, 14
Retail Foreign Exchange, 122
Retail Forex, 122
Reversal, 15, 122
Reversal Patterns, 11
Software, 53
Specialist, 121
Spinning Tops, 18
Stochastic Oscillator, 29, 102
Stock, 123
Stock Market, 123
Stock Quote, 123
Support, 123
Support and Resistance, 8, 14, 41
Support Turned Resistance, 15
Swing Trading, 37
Technical Analysis, 1, 4, 31, 109, 123
Technical Analysis Software, 47
Technical Indicators, 8, 27, 40, 55
TheFXperts, 114
Tick Chart, 123
Trade Plan, 33
Trade Signal Generating Software, 49
Trading Ranges, 34
Trading Robot, 51
Trading Signals, 39

Trading Software, 43
Trend, 123
Trend Lines, 13, 15
Trend Trading, 37
Trendline, 124
Triangles, 9, 12, 24
Triple Top, 12
Trough, 124

Volume, 124
Wedges, 10
Williams' %R, 106, *See* Williams' Percent Range
Williams' Percent Range, 105, 106
Zig-Zags, 23

www.ingramcontent.com/pod-product-compliance
Lightning Source LLC
Chambersburg PA
CBHW031922240526
45464CB00022B/643